10⁻

2

CONDITION: F-=/UG   (191082)

Edition: 1st   Prtg: DJ/NO

COMMENTS: Same

KEYWORDS: NO UNLISTED,

12.9

250 16

The
Fly-fisherman's
Workshop

Also by Loring D. Wilson:

The Handy Sportsman
The Edge of the River
Tying and Fishing the Terrestrials

South Brunswick and New York: A. S. Barnes and Company
London: Thomas Yoseloff Ltd

The Fly-fisherman's Workshop

Loring D. Wilson

A. S. Barnes and Co., Inc.
Cranbury, New Jersey 08512

Thomas Yoseloff Ltd
Magdalen House
136-148 Tooley Street
London SE1 2TT, England

Library of Congress Cataloging in Publication Data

Wilson, Loring D
  The fly-fisherman's workshop.

  Includes index.
  1. Fishing tackle—Design and construction. 2. Fly
fishing. I. Title.
SH447.W54   688.7′9   77-84594
ISBN 0-498-02182-3

PRINTED IN THE UNITED STATES OF AMERICA

To My Father and Mother

Clarence Wilson, who taught me the art of
angling, and whose hands could turn
a piece of wood into a work of art

and

Dorine Wilson, who taught me that the
written word was man's greatest
achievement

Contents

Introduction

Fishing with the long rod can be a very relaxing and rewarding sport, and, while the technique is hard to master at first, once the proper degree of skill is attained, fly-fishing can be one of the deadliest forms of angling in existence. On the surface, fly-fishing would seem to be a rather simple form of angling in terms of equipment, since the fly-fisherman is not burdened with a massive tackle box full of hardware that bristles with treble hooks, wire leaders, jars of pork rinds, bait boxes, minnow buckets, live bags, and all the other paraphernalia of the "conventional" fisherman.

Nothing could be further from the truth. The chief difference between the two types of fishing is that the fly-fisherman's gear is more or less miniaturized. His lures come in far greater variety, yet many of them are smaller than the barb on one of the hooks of a spin-fisherman's plug. And if anyone believes that fly-fishing is inexpensive, he has only to look through some of the catalogs of fly-tying and fly-fishing equipment. The tiny flies cost anywhere from 60¢ to $1.50 (sometimes higher for special patterns and salmon flies); fly lines run anywhere from $4.00 to $30.00; rods and reels can easily hit the three-figure mark; and, in addition, there are the waders, fly boxes, tapered leaders, creels, fishing vests, nets, wading staffs, fly floatant, and a host of small streamside tools that make the angler feel better equipped.

If the fly-fisherman ties his own flies he can bring the cost of the individual fly down to a few cents; but in order to do so he must purchase certain tools: fly-tying vise, scissors, hackle pliers, and a bodkin. Should he wish a better setup, there are bobbins to hold the thread, half-hitch tools and whip finishers to aid in the tying process, special

9

vises for nonstandard hooks, bobbin threaders, hackle guards, hackle gauges—the list goes on and on.

In addition there are the materials to be purchased: hairs and furs of all descriptions, feathers from more species of birds than I would care to name, hackles, latex rubber, corks, floss, tinsel, chenille, polypropylene yarn and dubbing, hooks, of all sizes and shapes—in the materials line the list is virtually endless, since flytiers are constantly inventing new patterns, and it seems as though each new pattern makes use of some new material—mylar piping, Duco cement, sponge rubber, balsa wood—well, you get the idea.

In short, it is an easy matter for a "well-equipped" fly-fisherman to have several thousand dollars invested in equipment of one sort or another. This is certainly not the average expenditure—although most fly-fishermen have several hundred dollars invested in equipment—but it serves to show that fly-fishing is not a cheap sport, at any rate.

This brings us to the purpose of *The Fly-fisherman's Workshop*. While there are certain items that a fly-fisherman must purchase, ready-made, such as reels, fly lines, waders, and certain fly-tying equipment, there are many others that, with a little ingenuity, and a little time, he can make for himself at considerable savings. They all will contribute to the enjoyment of the sport, especially since there is a certain extra satisfaction in using something that you have made with your own hands. This book will present those articles of equipment which can be made satisfactorily (and in some cases better than the commercially manufactured product) by anyone with a basic knowledge of tools.

In the first chapter we will take a look at the workshop itself and the tools necessary for the basic operations required for the projects in this book. But if you are reading this introduction in the bookstore while making up your mind, let me say at this point that in only one instance—the fly-tying vise—is a power tool required, although if you already own power tools they will make some of the operations easier. The tool required for the construction of the vise is a lathe, and if you do not have access to a lathe yourself, most woodworking shops will make the turning for you for about a dollar. Considering that fly-tying vises cost between eight and fifteen dollars, it is a small enough investment, since it will bring the total cost outlay for the vise to about three dollars.

This is *not* a book of fly-fishing techniques, nor will it tell you how to tie flies. Those subjects can be found in many other books. Rather, this is a book for the angler who has already discovered the pleasures of fly-fishing and who wants to expand his enjoyment of the sport, but whose budget does not permit merely purchasing all of the equipment he desires. In the same line of thought, it is neither a beginner's nor an expert's book. Rather, it is designed for any worker of the long rod. If your coordination allows you to present a fly with even a modicum of skill, it will permit you to build the projects presented here.

In addition, it provides something else. There are times when we have some time off from the daily battle, but circumstances prevent us from getting to the watery retreats that we love so well. To be able in those moments to work with our hands at creating something that we will take to the stream or lake, or carry to the fly-tying bench, not only gives us the satisfaction of creating something useful, it also allows us to extend our sport into another dimension. And the more dimensions a sport or hobby has, the more rewarding it becomes.

What do you lack? A wading staff? A tool to aid in tying parachute hackle flies? Do your waders leak? Is there a hole in your favorite trout net? Does your reel grind when you strip line? The solutions to these problems, and more, are in the pages that follow. But using this book is more than solving problems. It is fun.

The
Fly-fisherman's
Workshop

1

The Workshop

The workshop for the fly-fisherman can be simple or complex, depending upon how much time and money one wishes to devote to building his or her own tackle. All of the tools necessary for the projects listed in this book can be purchased for under $35.00, and many of them are probably already lying around the house or garage anyway. Should the builder desire power tools, the cost of the workshop can jump to as high a limit as the individual is willing to spend.

I will say this at the outset. If you only intend to build the projects listed in this book, do not go to extremes with the tools, or you will not save any money. The purchase value of the items described here comes to over $150.00 (and I am basing that price on the discount, mail-order catalog prices), while the cost of materials to build them will run about $25.00 or less, depending upon where you purchase your lumber, and in what quantities. Assuming that you have the common tools around the house, such as a saw, hammer, and pocketknife and a few others, your outlay for special tools will be in the neighborhood of $10.00. That means a total savings, if you build all the projects (and after you have seen them you will probably want to), of approximately $115.00, give or take a few dollars, not to mention the pleasure of doing the work yourself.

This is quite a substantial savings, but if you start adding power tools, special hobby knives, and the like, the savings will dwindle rapidly. You may desire two or three each of some of the projects in this book, but even so, before you go to "convenience" tools, decide whether you will be making the projects for personal satisfaction or monetary savings.

Saws

The first tool required is a saw. Since all of the construction-type projects are made of wood, a saw is the most important tool you will have, and I recommend three types to enable you to perform all of the operations required for project construction.

The crosscut saw is the mainstay of the woodworker's craft. It is designed for smooth cuts across the grain of the wood, but it will also handle rip cuts (cuts made along the line of the grain) quite nicely. Purchase a good one, because it will be used in eleven of the seventeen projects in the book. A good crosscut saw, 10 points to the inch, can be purchased for about $8.00, if you do not already have one, and since this is the most expensive tool you will need, as well as the tool you will need most often, there is no point in scrimping on its cost.

The crosscut saw is excellent for all straight cuts, but there are times when a curved cut is required, or when a finer cut is desired, as in the cutting of very thin pieces of wood that the crosscut saw might split. Those needs are best filled with a coping saw. The coping saw uses a very thin blade, and can be used to cut curves and scrolls, as well as

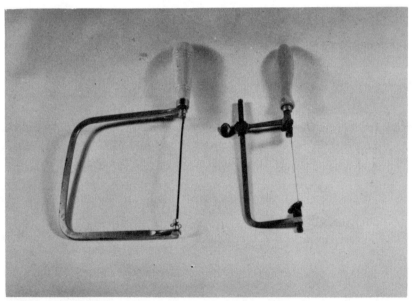

Coping and jeweler's saws

straight lines in very soft woods, such as balsa, which the larger teeth of the crosscut saw would shred. Coping saws cost in the neighborhood of two dollars, and extra blades cost a few cents apiece.

The third type of saw, a jeweler's saw, makes even finer cuts than the coping saw, and has the advantage of cutting small metal pieces so smooth that very little finishing is required. It is a handy little tool to have for very fine, critical tolerance work, and is extremely handy in making some of the fly-tying tools. The approximate cost is three dollars, and blades cost only slightly more than coping saw blades. If you purchase a jeweler's saw, get plenty of extra blades along with it, since the wire-thin blades break easily. If cost is really a problem, this is one of the few tools in this section that you can get by without.

Hammer

A hammer is next on the agenda. For the projects in this book any hammer will do, from the cheapest to the most expensive. I recommend a claw hammer, simply for ease in removing a misdirected or bent nail. If you happen to have some other sort of hammer lying around the garage, by all means use it, because nails can always be extracted with a pair of pliers.

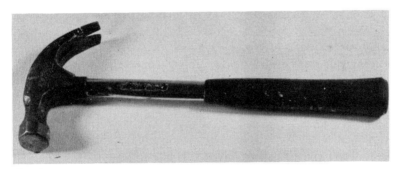

Claw hammer

Pliers

Pliers come next, and here the long-nosed, or needle-nosed pliers as they are sometimes called, are the ones to buy. Again, no real quality is necessary here, and pliers can sometimes be found in those "Any Tool—79¢" displays in supermarkets and hardware stores that will suffice quite nicely. They will serve double duty later if you are also a

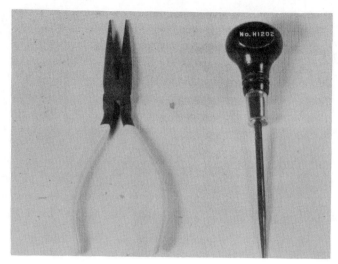

Long-nosed pliers and awl

flytier, because they can be used to flatten lead wrappings on hooks to create the natural, flat-bodied nymphs that have become so popular in recent years.

Screwdrivers

Small screwdrivers are also required on some of the projects, and here again you can probably find what you need at the supermarket

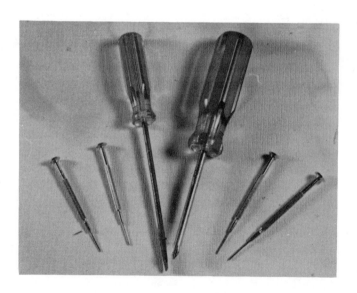

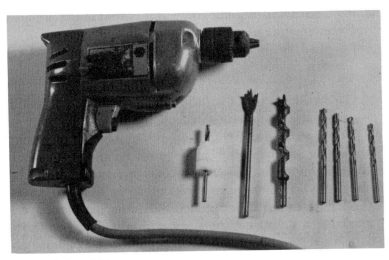

Power drill and bits

tool table. Sometimes you can even find sets of five or six screwdrivers for under a dollar. They are not much good for fine cabinetry, but they are more than ample for a fly-fisherman's workshop. If you happen to see a cheap set of what are called "jeweler's screwdrivers" at the same table, and you have an extra dollar, by all means add them. They are not necessary, but the very small blades come in handy sometimes in repairing reels and other equipment that is put together with tiny screws.

Drill

The single power tool that you should own is a ¼ " power drill. They can be obtained for ten dollars or less—less than the cost of a good crosscut saw—and they make starting screws and boring holes for the installation of dowels much easier than attempting the same operations with a hand drill. In addition, an inexpensive power drill costs *less* than a decent hand drill, and will perform more varied operations, such as sanding and buffing. With the addition of special auger bits, it will also double for the brace and bit. Unless you want a complete set of drills for other projects around the house, purchase the bits singly, as they are needed. And, when you purchase your drill, add the expense of a drill stop. This is a small plastic device that attaches to the bit itself, to keep the bit from going past a predetermined depth—a very necessary item when making the fly-drying rack and the line-storage rack, as well as coming in handy in several other projects. Drill stops cost less than 50¢ at this writing, and you will save that much in the avoidance of ruined wood alone.

Plane

Unless you are highly adept with a plane, purchase one of the handy Surform tools, a trade name for a cross between a plane and a rasp— excellent for removing wood quickly, for primary finishing before sandpaper, or for shaping rod and net handles. A four-faced rasp is worth having, but the Surform is easier to use, since the teeth of the tool do not clog up the way the teeth of a rasp will, and it does not require the skill necessary to use a plane effectively. It also does not have to be resharpened, for if it ever gets dull (I have been using one for almost three years and it cuts as cleanly as it did when it was brand new) you can obtain replacement blades for it at nominal cost.

The Surform tool comes in various sizes and shapes, a few of which are shown in the illustration. The two handiest styles are the standard, flat rasp/plane type, and the curved, or half-round type, used primarily for cutting the rough outline of the curves into the handle of your fly rod. Surforms cost between $1.50 and $3.00 each, so purchase as many different styles as you can afford, but by all means get the flat and the curved.

Various surform tools

Knives

Next on your list of tools is a good pocketknife. The one I use is called a Stockman's Knife, and the three blade styles take care of almost all my cutting needs. Get a good knife at the outset—preferably one with high carbon steel rather than stainless steel blades. The stainless looks prettier longer, and you do not have to worry as much about rust, but all knives get dull eventually, and it is much—and I mean much—harder to restore a good, sharp edge to a stainless steel blade than it is to a carbon steel blade. Keep the knife sharp, use it only for your workshop, wipe the blades with oil after each use (put a drop on the hinges as well), teach your spouse the difference between a knife and a screwdriver, and do not let the kids get hold of it, and a good pocketknife will give excellent service for a lifetime. I will not go into brands here—I will just say that, in my experience, any pocketknife that costs less than five dollars is money thrown away. As in the case of most things in this world of ours, you get what you pay for.

Awl

The next tool used in these projects is an awl. Basically an awl is simply a sharpened steel rod set in a handle, and used for punching holes in canvas, leather, cardboard, and other thin materials. It can also be used to "drill" holes in balsa wood by rotating it between the hands while applying pressure against the wood. Awls generally cost less than a dollar, and can also be used for "burnishing" small pieces of metal, reaming small holes in plastic, and tapering the inside of small plastic tubing—a very versatile and very inexpensive tool.

Hand Stitcher

The final tool is a hand stitcher. Hand stitchers are basically sewing

Sewing awl

21

tools, and will be used in making the canvas creel and in a few operations on the fly-fisherman's vest. They cost about $2.00, and may not be readily obtainable at many hardware stores. However, they are available from the Netcraft Company, and some sporting-goods specialties stores carry them. They consist of a replaceable needle and a spool of heavy, waxed nylon thread in a hollow wooden handle, and go under various brand names. Hand stitchers form a lock stitch, like a sewing machine, but can be used on heavy materials that would break a sewing machine. With the hand stitcher in your workshop, once you clip all the hair off that old deerskin to use as hair bugs, shave the skin with a razor, get yourself a pattern, and make a pair of moccasins to wear when you are sitting around the camp after a good day's fishing.

Other Tools

There are a few other odds and ends that could be called tools that you should have available, and that you probably have already. The first is a ruler for making straight lines on the lumber. A metal ruler is best, since the edge is perfectly smooth and perfectly straight, but plastic or wood is sufficient. A supply of pencils with standard leads (not the hard, draftsman's pencils—the lines do not show up well enough) should be on hand, so that if the lead in one pencil breaks, you do not have to drop everything and run to the pencil sharpener.

Single-edged razor blades are essential for cutting balsa wood, trimming canvas, cutting plastic, and a host of other small cutting jobs where a very fine and exceptionally sharp blade is required. If you

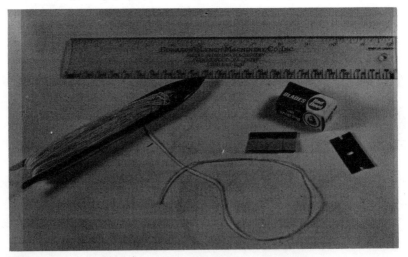

Miscellaneous tools: ruler single-edge razors and shuttle

make cork-bodied bass bugs—in fact, if you tie flies at all—you probably have some already. If not, they cost about a nickel apiece. Make sure you get the ones designed for paint scrapers, with a plate of steel bent over one edge of the blade. These are the safest available.

A net-tying shuttle is handy for repairing tears in trout or bass nets, since it can be carried fully loaded with twine in the bottom of a tackle box or in a pocket. They cost about 25¢ apiece from Netcraft, Herters, and various other companies. Nets can be repaired with a simple length of twine, however, so the shuttle, unless you decide to make your own nets, is merely a convenience tool—albeit a very inexpensive one.

That about takes care of the tools you will be needing. In the realm of materials, the necessities for each project will be listed at the beginning of the specific chapter. There are certain generalizations that can be made, however, to give you an idea of some of the things with which to stock your workshop.

Wood

Wood is used in more than half the projects in this book. For the most part you will be using standard 1″ white pine, available at any lumberyard. I will not get into the confusing issue of lumber measurements here. In only one of the projects—the fly-fisherman's tackle box —would they be of any issue, and I will explain what is necessary in that chapter when we come to it.

In the case of the fly-storage boxes, you will be using aromatic cedar, and in some of the other projects, balsa wood and a few small pieces of other types of lumber. Many, if not all, of these can be obtained in hobby shops across the country. Prices for the small amounts you will be using are nominal, and in some cases, where a particular wood that I have used may be difficult to obtain, I have listed alternative choices that will do the job as well.

Needless to say, you will not be purchasing wood in advance, but there are several materials that you should have on the shelf before you start the projects. Those materials, both types and amounts, are as follows:

Glue: Four types

1. White glue—this is the standard for gluing wood. It is water soluble, so it is easy to clean up, and it dries clear. When using white glue, wipe the project down with a wet cloth after gluing. This will

prevent excess glue from drying on the outside of the projects and interfering with their finish. It has the added advantage of raising the grain for finish sanding. White glue comes in several types—Elmer's and Weldbond are both excellent. You shoud have a pint on hand.

2. Waterproof (Marine) glue—this is a plastic resin type of glue, a dry powder that is mixed with warm water and then applied. It is the same sort of glue that is used on boats, and the type that should be used in constructing the tackle box. Only a small amount should be mixed at a time, following the instructions on the label carefully. Since it is used only on the tackle box, the smallest can available—generally about two ounces—is sufficient.

3. Model cement—the glue used for building model airplanes and the like. It is used on some of the fly-tying tools, and on the fly boxes. Both Ambroid and Duco cement are fine glues. Model cement must be applied very sparingly, since cleanup is extremely difficult. This glue is also flammable, so due care should be exercised in using it. One tube will be enough for the projects in this book.

4. Ferrule cement—this is a very particular cement used to glue tip tops and ferrules onto the fly rod. It is handy to carry in the tackle box for rod repair. It comes in stick form, and can be obtained from any company that sells rod-making supplies, as well as from most sporting-goods stores. Ferrule cement is heated with a match to melt it enough to use, and it dries very quickly. One stick is plenty, and will last for several years—or several rods, whichever comes first.

White and waterproof glues

Oils and cements

Nails

Nails are next on the agenda as fasteners. Since all of the woodworking projects are relatively small, and all should have a decent finish, you will be using only two types of nails: finishing nails and brads. In the field of finishing nails, purchase a pound of 6d (abbreviation for "six-penny"), and a pound of 4d. These will be more than enough. For the brads, which are merely very small finishing nails, a package of ½ " and a package of 1" brads will suffice. In addition, a package of dressmaker's pins is handy to have for pinning balsa and some plastics together while the glue is drying, and will be necessary when making the fly-fishing vest and the canvas creel.

Sandpaper

Garnet paper gives the best finish on wood, although it does not last as long as some of the other varieties available. Ten sheets each in 80, 120, and 220 grit will be enough. You should also have a few sheets of medium-grade emery cloth for touching up metal surfaces.

Steel Wool

Always use steel wool after the 220 grit garnet paper to give a glass-smooth finish. If the project is wiped with a damp cloth, little "whiskers" of wood will be raised, which the steel wool will take off. Steel wool is also good for polishing metal and cleaning ferrules and should always be used in between coats of varnish to assure the smoothest finish possible. A few packages of "assortments" from 00 to 0000 grade will take care of your needs.

Oil

One can of 3-in-1 or a good grade of gun oil should always be on hand. It is used in cleaning, repairing, and servicing equipment, and in making sure that the tools you are using stay in good condition.

Grease

Reel grease is what is called for here, and a tube should always be at hand, whether in the shop or at streamside. It can mean the difference between a smoothly operating reel and a bound-up spool of line that you cannot use.

Varnish

Whether you stain your wooden projects or not, they should all be finished with three or four coats of varnish. Varnish not only gives them a better appearance, it protects them from water and other minor surface damage. For several years now I have been using a product called Zar, an acrylic coating that positively does not yellow even when constantly exposed to sunlight, and that does not crack when subjected to knocks and scrapes. Even if you drop a rock on it, the finish will dent rather than scratch or crack. It is expensive, but I feel it is well worth the price. If Zar is unavailable, a good grade of marine, or spar, varnish will also do an excellent job. Whichever you use, a quart will be sufficient.

That takes care of the general shop set-up. Small items like hinges and other hardware will be covered as they are required. With the shop set up as outlined above, you will have spent—possibly—$30.00. You still have a little to spend, and a lot to save. You also have a lot of fun and personal pride ahead of you. Your only problem now will be deciding what to build first. May all your problems be that small.

2

Building the Fly Rod

It seems as though a fly-fisherman never has quite enough fly rods. We may start out with a medium weight, 8' or 8½', "trout action" rod, and some of us may find it sufficient for many years. But once the challenge of fly-fishing takes hold, we start seeking other species of fish with the long rod, and we find that there are limitations to being a single-rod angler. So there comes a time when a short rod is needed for delicate presentation of midges to gin-clear, low-water trout; when a rod with a heavier, stiffer action is necessary to present the heavy, wind-resistant bugs to lily-pad largemouths; when an even beefier rod is sought to handle battling salmon; and, when freshwater seasons or locales are unavailable, the behemoth of the long rods is called for to handle the behemoths of the sea.

Needless to say, the expense of a rod of each type is prohibitive to all but affluent anglers: listed above are only five separate rod types, yet within those types there are subtle differences in length, strength, and stiffness, so that the choice of combinations is tremendous. But there is a means by which the average angler can afford to own several rods. He can build them himself.

With the advent of fiberglass rods, rod construction on the personal level became practical. And while a fiberglass rod may not have the aesthetic value of a split bamboo, the action, now that the bugs have been worked out of fiberglass construction, is equally as good—in some cases, if I may be permitted a small heresy, better, especially in the realm of bass and saltwater rods.

Fiberglass rods are really quite simple to build, once you get the hang of it, and there are two ways of going about it. The first is to purchase a kit, which contains all of the parts necessary, from the blank to the reel seat; the second is to purchase the component parts separately, and proceed from scratch. The latter method certainly makes for a more personal, individual rod. Nevertheless, knowing precisely what is necessary comes only with practice—different brands of guides last longer, some operations can be made less expensive but at the cost of far greater working time, and certain parts of the rod equipment—the ferrules, the tip top, and the reel seat—must be geared toward a particular blank or you will run into extreme problems. I will explain rod construction from scratch later in this chapter, but I strongly recommend that your first one or two rods be built from a kit. In that way, you will know that all sizes are correct, and you will gain the practical experience of putting a rod together without having to worry about odd-sized parts and adapting a rod to take them.

Kits are available from many sources. At the time of this writing, for three of the major sellers of kits, prices (approximate) are as follows: The Netcraft Company—$9.00 to $11.00; Herter's—$11.00 to $17.00; and E. Hille—$14.00 to $29.00. In addition, Herter's currently supplies kits with an extra tip section at a slightly higher cost, and Hille offers kits based on the new, excellent, and expensive graphite rod blanks, at prices between $85.00 and $110.00 for the kit—a savings over ready-made graphite rods, certainly (at present, Fly Fisherman's Bookcase and Tackle Service is selling Fenwick graphite rods for between $115.00 and $187.50), but still a bit too rich for the tastes of most of us.

By far the greatest value for the money lies in fiberglass rod kits. To a certain extent, you get what you pay for, but I have been using one of Netcraft's cheapest rod kits for years, and I have never found fault with either its durability or its action. If you tend to break rod tips with any sort of frequency, the Herter's kit with the extra tip may be to your advantage, since you will be assured of having an extra tip that will match the butt section both in blank color and windings color. Netcraft sells extra tip sections, however, so the choice of initial cost is ultimately up to you.

The bill of materials includes basically the rod kit and a few tools, but to make things simpler for the person who wants to start from scratch (or go on to a "from scratch" rod after a few kits) the bill presented here lists the individual components needed to build a fly rod, and the tools required, both for kit building, and for individual component construction.

Bill of Materials: Building the Fly Rod	
MATERIALS	TOOLS
Fiberglass rod blank (length to suit)	For Kit:
Cork rings (or preformed cork grip)	Rod winder (or heavy book)
Reel seat	Razor blade
Winding check	Coping saw
Ferrule set	6″ copper wire
Snake guide set	4″ glass square
Hook keeper	Popsicle stick
Rod winding thread	
Color preservative	
Rod varnish	Tools for rod from scratch are same as for
Ferrule cement	use with kit
Epoxy cement	
Sandpaper	

For your first kit rod, I strongly suggest purchasing a kit that comes with a preformed grip rather than the separate cork rings. We shall be dealing with making a grip from cork rings when we talk about building the rod from the beginning, but using a preformed grip on your first rod will enable you to concentrate on just putting the rod together properly rather than having to worry about shaping.

Kits come with the rod blank already cut into sections, and the ferrules sized to fit perfectly. The first step, therefore, is to install the ferrules on the rod blank. Heat the ferrule cement and apply it liberally to the end of the blank, keeping it soft. Now heat the ferrules and press them snugly over the ends of the blank with a slight twisting motion to spread the cement evenly. Press them as tightly as they will go, but do *not* use pliers, due to the possibility of deforming the ferrules or scratching them. Allow the ferrule cement to dry for fifteen or twenty minutes before doing anything else to the rod.

Some kits recommend the use of epoxy for ferrules and tip top. I do not. Admittedly, the epoxy gives a longer-lasting bond—but after many years, should the tip top become rough or the ferrules recalcitrant, they cannot be removed without cutting the rod back—and that means that you will not be able to get new ferrules to fit. With ferrule cement, all you need to do is heat the damaged metalwork with a cigarette lighter and twist it off, and you will be able to install a new set.

Incidentally, here is a little hint that has nothing to do with actually building the rod, but that can save you a lot of grief on the stream. Before you install the tip top, measure the diameter of the rod approximately three inches back from the tip of the blank, and order another tip top of *that* diameter. After your rod is built, put the remainder of the ferrule cement and the larger tip top in one of your fly boxes or your vest—anyplace that you will always have it with you. Then, should the delicate tip of the rod snap on the stream, it is an easy matter to cut the tip back to the measured area with a pocketknife and glue on the new tip top—and you are back in business again.

After the ferrules are hard, install the cork grip with epoxy cement. Install it so that the measurement between the end of the grip and the butt of the blank is ¼ " less than the length of the reel seat. The grip should make a snug fit; if it does not, wrap thread through the epoxy, making certain that there is still plenty of cement oozing out on top of it, and trying the grip periodically until the grip is snug. Let the grip assembly dry for twenty-four hours (or however long your particular brand of epoxy recommends).

After the cement is thoroughly dry, determine the spine of the rod. All rod blanks have a spine, or stiff line, and the spines of both sections must match if the rod is to be accurate in casting. Luckily, the spine is easy enough to locate. Simply lean the rod so that one end is on the floor and the other on a table or some other straight, smooth surface. Now roll the blank slowly with the palm of your hand. You will feel the stiff spot as the rod flexes with your hand midway between the table edge and the floor. Mark the stiff point with a small pencil line right at the edge of the ferrule on both parts of the blank. Now put the ferrules together, and lay the rod in a cradle (use the rod wrapping tool described at the end of this chapter) so that the pencil lines are facing straight up.

With the lines straight up, install the tip top with ferrule cement, and the reel seat with epoxy, forcing the end of the seat ¼ " into the cork grip. Allow both to dry overnight. The trickiest part of the rod is now finished.

All that really remains now is to install the guides. Each kit comes with a set of guides designed for it, and instructions telling you how far apart they should be mounted. Since this varies from blank to blank, and from manufacturer to manufacturer, follow their instructions.

Making certain that the guide is in perfect line with the tip top, tape one leg of the guide to the blank. Tape one end of the thread to the blank with a very small piece of tape, ½ " from the end of the other foot of the guide. Now, holding the winding thread under tension, either with a rod winding bobbin, or by passing it through the pages of a heavy book, start revolving the rod in the cradle so that the thread is laid onto the rod smoothly and tightly, each turn right against the last. Watch the wrapping carefully; if there is a small gap, and no more than two or three turns have been wrapped after it occurred, the gap can be closed by pushing it together with the thumbnail.

Wind tightly right up to the foot of the guide.

One of the problems that beginners have with wrapping a rod occurs at this point—a gap in the thread where the thickness of the guide foot interferes with the wrapping. It can be easily avoided in this manner: As soon as the foot of the guide is reached, wrap four or five loose turns of thread over the leg of the guide, without worrying about gaps. Then, holding tension on the thread, use your thumbnail to slide the thread down the leg of the guide until it butts up against the previous wrappings. The thread will act like a sort of sock, and cover the foot of the guide without gaps.

Continue wrapping, tightly, until approximately six turns from the point at which the guide bends upward. Take a six-inch length of copper wire and bend it in the middle. Lay the loop across the windings with the closed end opposite the guide. Now wrap tightly the last six or seven turns, *over* the loop. Holding tension on the thread, cut the thread so that there is a three-inch "tail." Slip this free end through the copper loop, grab the two exposed ends of the wire, and pull. The loop will draw the thread through with it, burying the end under six or seven turns of thread. Cut the end off flush with a single-edged razor blade.

Remove the tape from the other foot of the guide, and wrap it in the same manner. Continue with the rest of the guides, always making certain that they are in alignment before you start—you cannot change the alignment once the guides are wrapped. Install the hook keeper close to the grip in the same manner.

At this time you may add whatever decorative wrappings you wish, or leave the rod as it is. Some wrappings give the rod a distinctive or individual air, but too many can detract from its appearance. I once witnessed an angler on a small stream on Maryland's Eastern Shore whose rod was so thoroughly wrapped with stripes and crosses in such a wide array of colors that it looked like a tall, skinny Egyptian mummy dressed up for the Junior Prom. Decorate as you desire, but *please* use some restraint!

After all the guides are wrapped, apply color preservative liberally to the windings. If you do not saturate them thoroughly, they will discolor when the varnish is applied.

Apply the varnish with the fingers, twirling the rod as you do. It makes your hands messy, but you do not get drips and runs in the rod that way. Two coats are generally sufficient to protect the rod, and I recommend, although it is not technically necessary, a good coat of paste wax. It helps to protect the rod from the elements (especially if the rod is to be used in salt or brackish water), and it is easier to apply another coat of wax than another coat of varnish. Get the wax from an auto shop, and ask for the kind used on fiberglass car bodies. The smallest can available will last for years.

There is not that much difference between building a rod from scratch and building one from a kit. Because of the length of fly rods, almost all blanks are shipped already cut, and if you request, the supplier will generally sell you the proper ferrules for the rod blank in question, or, should he not carry the hardware, at least inform you of the proper size to purchase. In the event that you purchase a one-piece blank, invest in an accurate vernier caliper at the same time, so that you can measure the precise diameter of the ends of the sections after you have cut the rod with the jeweler's saw or a very fine blade in the coping saw. And, if you cannot afford, or cannot find, the caliper, then make the most accurate measurement you can with tools at hand, and order that sized ferrule plus the next largest and the next smallest. With any reliable supplier, if you explain your purpose, he will generally let you return the unneeded ferrules—but find out in advance. The only advantage that I can see in purchasing a one-piece blank is that, if you have the facilities to carry it, you can end up with a one-piece rod that will not have any flat spots in the action caused by the ferrules; or, if you have a very small car or are going a long way by bicycle or on foot, as in wilderness camping and fishing, you can custom-make your own multipiece pack rod.

All procedures for the "from scratch" rod are the same as for building the kit rod, with the exception of the grip. Of course, it is possible to purchase preformed grips, in which case nothing whatsoever is different. But for a truly customized rod—one that feels exactly the way you want it to when you hold it—you may be interested in shaping the grip yourself from cork rings. For those so interested, the procedure is as follows:

Purchase cork rings with the smallest hole diameter available. A wooden dowel wrapped with sandpaper is used to ream out the hole to the proper diameter for the butt of the rod, but proceed slowly, since holes that are too large cannot be effectively mounted. If anything, the hole should be a trifle too small, since cork will compress somewhat when forced onto the blank, to provide a very snug fit.

The common length for fly-rod handle grips is 7″, which requires 14 cork rings (standard thickness is ½″). Add to this the length of the reel seat, and purchase enough rings to make the total length (do not subtract ¼″ this time, because the end of the reel seat will not be inset into the grip). If you plan to make several rods, purchase the rings in bulk, because they are much cheaper by the hundred; otherwise plan the length exactly, and order that many rings plus 2; the extra rings are in case of damaging one by accident, or for later repair.

Ream the holes to proper diameter one at a time as you proceed to lessen the chance of mistakes. Now coat the bottom ½" of the blank with model airplane cement, and force the first cork ring down over it, twisting it slightly to spread the glue. Coat the next ½" of the blank, *plus* the upper side of the cork ring, with cement, and install the next ring in the same manner, pressing it tightly against the ring below it. Continue in this manner until all the rings have been glued into place. If the fit of the rings is snug enough--and it should be--there will be no need to clamp the rings, because the tension will hold them tightly in place until the glue dries.

The rings will not be in perfect alignment, since the holes in them are very seldom exactly dead center, but this does not really matter, since the offsets will be removed when the grip is shaped.

After the glue has dried overnight, use a rasp or Surform tool to take the excess cork off the rings, reducing it to a relatively even cylinder. The top fourteen rings will form the grip. With the Surform and coarse sandpaper reduce all rings below those fourteen to the inside diameter of the reel seat. Proceed slowly, since this fit *must* be snug.

After the base for the reel seat is finished, shape the grip to your own liking, either by duplicating that of a favorite rod, or by creating your own. Shape with progressively finer grades of sandpaper, rather than a rasp, since at this point too much cork removed will cause all the work to have been wasted. 50 grit is a good coarseness for starting; work down to 220. For concave curves, wrap the sandpaper around your finger rather than a dowel; it will provide a smoother curve, and it is much easier to gauge the pressure you are applying.

After the grip has been shaped and is satin smooth, coat the base for the reel seat with glue and install the seat, aligning it with the spine of the rod as in the case of the kit. Allow it to dry for twenty-four hours, and then proceed with the rest of the rod making just as described in the previous pages.

While I recommend that the first attempt at rod building be through the use of a kit, because of the fact that everything is pre-selected and fitted, there are certain advantages to building rods from scratch. As mentioned above, the angler can wind up with a rod of either one piece or many pieces, depending upon personal need. In addition, for the angler who flings feathers for various species, and who needs several different types of rod, there is considerable savings to be had by purchasing in bulk. Not only are cork rings less expensive, but the blanks themselves are frequently sold in lots of three at a cost equivalent to two purchased individually, as are sets of guides and reel seats. This breaks down, in effect, to purchasing two rods and getting one free, not to mention the tremendous savings over purchasing already finished rods. And, by building the rods from scratch, the angler can choose special types of guides (single-footed, carbide, chromed, etc., depending upon the use for which the rod is intended), and choose his own color combination for thread rather than accepting the kit maker's color choice.

All in all, building rods is quite simple, and quite inexpensive. The blanks are usually the same as those used in some well-known brand, although the rod builder seldom finds out unless he purchases directly from that company, and then he pays extra for the name. But having a battery of ten rods, and being able to meet all contingencies, for less than the cost of a single graphite or bamboo wand, is quite a lot to gain for simply giving up a manufacturer's name on a rod. Put your own on it. All the custom rod makers do, and a custom rod—especially one you have made yourself—is something to cause very justifiable pride.

Rod Wrapping Cradle

One of the chief problems faced by beginning rod builders is wrapping on the guides, and that problem relates to the matter of supporting the rod evenly while it is turned. There are many commercial cradles on the market that support the rod, but they cost anywhere between $8.00 and $50.00, depending upon their complexity. There are also instructions available in some books that explain how you can create a motorized cradle for wrapping on the guides that will both support and turn the blank, so that all you have to worry about is guiding the thread.

These motorized wrappers are truly marvelous—if you happen to be building an average of fifteen or twenty rods per year. Let's face it: fingers were created for the sole purpose of creating flies and turning rods while we wrap them—that is the reason we have an opposing thumb. And since an excellent rod wrapping cradle—the one you are about to build—can be built in twenty minutes with thirty cents worth of material (only half the price of a pack of cigarettes), I can see no reason to avoid doing what our hands were created to do.

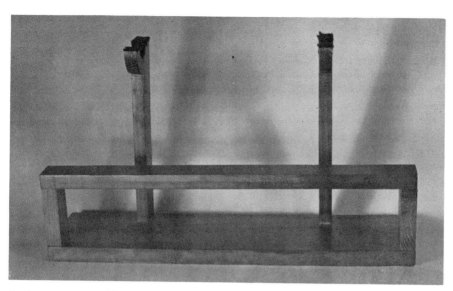

Rod-wrapping cradle

Bill of Materials		
1 pc. 1 x 5″ pine, 18″ long		Base
2 pc. 1 x 2″ pine, 3″ long		Supports
1 pc. 1 x 2″ pine, 18″ long		Bobbin shelf
1 pc. 1 x 3″ pine, 20″ long		Rod supports
2 pc. felt, ¾″ x 4″		Cradle liners
1 pc. felt, 5″ x 18″ (optional)		Bottom pad

Cut all pieces to the proper size, and sand all except the piece for the rod supports glass smooth. Assemble the supports to the base, flush with each end and one side, as shown in the diagram. Apply white glue to the base of each support, position it properly, and drive two 6d (six-penny) finishing nails into the bottom of the support through the base.

Apply glue to the tops of the supports, and place the bobbin shelf on top of them, lining the edges up flush. For appearance's sake, if you have C-clamps, simply clamp the shelf in place until it is dry with a piece of scrap wood between the shelf and the foot of the clamp to prevent marring. It is not necessary, but it prevents nail holes in the top of the shelf. If clamps are not available, simply nail the shelf to the tops of the supports after applying the glue.

The reason for not sanding the rod supports at the outset is that some wood has to be cut away, and there is no sense in sanding all your scraps. Divide the piece in half, crosswise, with a pencil line,

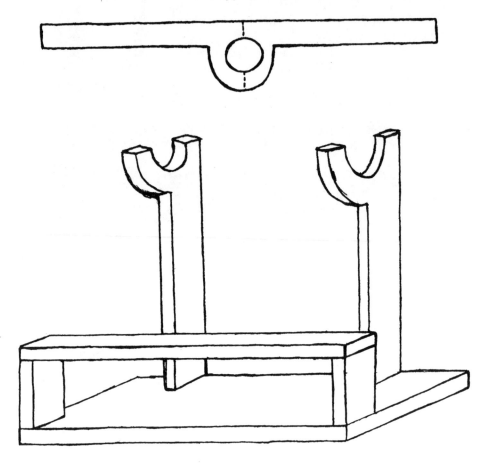

so that there are two marked off pieces that measure 1 x 3 x 10", but do not cut them yet. With a 1" wood bit in your power drill, bore a hole in the piece, centering it on the pencil line (see illustration). You form both halves of the cradle, with perfect semicircular curves, in that manner.

Now draw the pattern for the supports on the board as shown in the drawing, and cut away the waste wood. All the cutting can be accomplished with the coping saw, but you may find it easier to use the crosscut saw for the straight cuts while using the coping saw only for the curve. Then simply cut along your first pencil line to create the two 10" cradled rod supports. Sand them as smooth as the rest of the wood in your project.

Apply white glue to the bases of the two supports and position them flush with the back of the base, and 4" from each end. Fix them into place with two 6d finishing nails per support, driven through the underside of the base as in the case of the shelf supports.

The rod wrapping cradle may be left unfinished, or it may be stained and varnished, depending upon your preference. Should you desire to finish it, do so before installing the felt, since the stain and varnish will penetrate the felt otherwise and harden it, eliminating the cushioning effect.

After the finish has dried, install the two ¾ x 4″ pieces of felt in the cradles with white glue, covering all exposed wood. This felt is essential, since it will protect the blank from being scratched or otherwise abraded by the rough wood. The 5″ x 18″ piece of felt is optional, depending upon where you will be using the cradle. If outside, in a shop or on a workbench, it can be eliminated. If inside, on a table or some other piece of finished furniture, glue it to the bottom of the base to prevent the wrapping cradle from scratching the furniture.

Attach the wrapping bobbin (they cost less than $1.00, and are a worthwhile investment) to the shelf with the thread coming through the lower part of the bobbin toward you, and start wrapping. If you do not want to purchase the bobbin—you should—lay a book on the base, put a finishing nail in the shelf to hold the spool of thread, and run the thread through the pages of the book.

3

Fly-fisherman's Tackle Box

A tackle box? For fly-fishermen? No, it is not heresy, no matter what your traditional background. In the days when the fly rod was used primarily for trout and salmon in clear, crystalline streams, and wading was the only way of fishing, a tackle box was out of place. It was heavy, it got in the way, and it could not be carried along as the angler made his way from pool to riffle, fishing all the way. So special vests were developed to carry the fly boxes and other gear; for the trout purist, turn to page 54 and you will find what you need.

But today the fly rod is a very versatile piece of equipment, used for everything from panfish and bass to sailfish and tarpon—and in many instances, especially in reservoir bass fishing and saltwater angling, you cannot get to the fish on foot. You need a boat, and if you are in a boat you need some sort of flotation jacket, most of which are too bulky to permit the use of a fishing vest over them.

A tackle box solves the problem of the boat-bound fly-fisherman, but to date none of the major tackle companies (or the minor ones, for that matter) have seen fit to develop a box properly suited to our needs. The answer, obviously, is to build our own.

The fly-fisherman's tackle box has the advantage of being able to be varied to suit the needs of the individual angler, but all construction aspects are the same. The box described in this chapter is not only a very attractive piece of fishing furniture in its own right, but is quite effective, in that it holds five standard Perrine or Wheatley fly boxes

Fly-fisherman's tackle box

(for a total of over one thousand flies, depending upon the type of box used), plus two filled reels, leaders, and additional small equipment. There is also a rack in the lid of the box for drying wet flies.

Construction is actually quite simple if you follow the instructions carefully, and the capacity of the box can be increased simply by increasing the length of the sides, top, and bottom pieces.

Bill of Materials	
2 pc. pine, exact measurement ¾″ x 7″ x 13½″	Top and bottom
2 pc. ½″ x 4″ x 13½″ pine (exact)	Sides
2 pc. ½″ x 4″ x 6¼″ pine (exact)	Ends
2 Brass hinges	
1 Brass hasp-type latch	
1 Brass handle	
8 pc. ¼″ x ¼″ x 3½″ balsa	Fly box dividers
1 pc. ⅛″ cork to line top of box	
2 pc. ¼″ x ¼″ x 6¼″ balsa	Fly-drying rack

Begin by assembling the sides, ends, top, and bottom pieces as shown in the diagram, with the end pieces inside of the sides and the top and bottom overlapping both ends and sides. Assemble with glue and 4d finishing nails. When nailing the sides to the ends, place one of the nails ½″ below the upper edge, the next nail 1¼″ below the upper edge, and then space the rest evenly, using only enough to draw the glued surfaces smoothly together with no gaps.

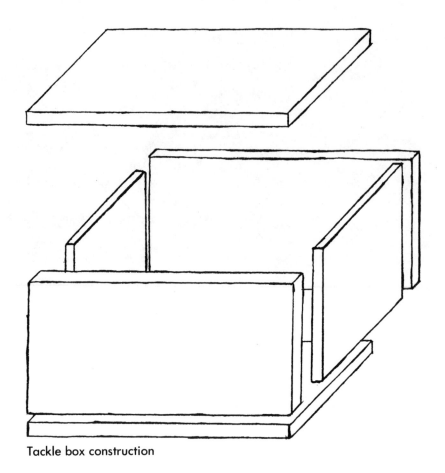

Tackle box construction

You now have a tackle box that the wife of any fisherman would adore, since you cannot get into it, but we will remedy that situation. The reason for building the entire box in a single piece is that it is very difficult to build a separate lid and bottom and have them fit perfectly —and a perfect fit is what is necessary to create a box that is both functional and beautiful.

Measure 7/8″ down from the top of the side pieces (1⅝″ from the top of the assembled box) and make a pencil mark. Do this on all four sides of the box, making a mark at the end of each board, and then join the marks with straight pencil lines. You should now have a single line that completely girdles the box. If the line is off at any junction, erase it, remeasure, and draw it again.

Place the box on its side and, using the crosscut saw, begin cutting through the box at one corner. Take special care that the blade of the saw follows the line on both the side and end at the same time; if it does not, the lid of the box will be uneven, and in addition to looking horrible it will not open and close properly, and the wood will have been wasted. Making the cut is a slow process, but it is the hardest part of making the tackle box, so once it is done everything else is smooth sailing.

When the blade first breaks through the other side of the box, turn it over and follow *that* line, again checking constantly to make certain that the blade follows all four lines evenly. Continue cutting until the box is divided into two open trays, one shallow (the lid), the other deep (the bottom of the box.) Now you see the reason for the positioning of the first two nails in each side—random placing might have gotten one or more nails in the path of the saw blade, an occurrence that would have been bad for the box, the teeth of the saw, and your blood pressure as well.

Use the Surform tool at this point to round all edges and corners with the exception of the edges of the two trays that fit together. The rounding is not necessary, but it makes a better finish for the box, and eliminates the future possibility of the finished box snagging clothing, nets, and other soft materials. Put the two parts of the box together, and start sanding, first with 80 grit paper, working down to 220 grit. Garnet paper works the best on this box, since the grains themselves wear down as you sand, making the paper itself progressively finer. By the time you have finished with the 220 grit, the box should feel as smooth as glass.

It is not, however. Some of the fine fibers of the wood have actually been compressed, and as soon as you apply stain they will swell and pop back up again, ruining the final finish. So, take a cloth dampened

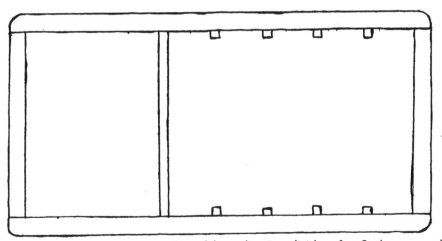

Tackle box construction: interior of box showing dividers for fly boxes, reel compartment

with warm (not hot) water, and wipe all exposed surfaces of the box. The moisture will raise the grain in tiny, hairlike extrusions. Use steel wool to go over the box after it has dried. Repeat the dampening and steel wooling one more time, and the box should feel slick to the touch. You are now ready to adapt it to the purposes of the fly-fisherman.

Choose the side of the box that has the most pleasing grain structure. This will be the front. On the other side install the two hinges. The ⅝" wide ornamental hinges used on the box in the photograph, built to the specifications expressed in this chapter, are placed exactly 2¼" from each end to create the proper balance for the lid. Larger hinges may have a somewhat different positioning point, but they should be evenly spaced so that the lid lifts smoothly.

Close the lid of the box and install the latch in the center of the front. Make it tight so that the lid does not move when it is latched. Install the handle on the top of the box, and the external construction work is completed.

Now open the tackle box, and install the fly box dividers with model airplane cement, forcing pins through them far enough to hold them firmly against the inside of the box while the cement dries. Since different fly boxes have different thicknesses, determine the exact positioning by actually using your fly boxes as your measuring tool. Place the first box against one end of the box, and cement and pin the first pair of dividers to the tackle box, just barely touching the fly box. Remove the box (so that none of the cement adheres to the fly box), and set your next one lightly against the pinned dividers, and pin the next set in. Proceed in this manner until all of the dividers have been pinned in place.

Now set the fifth (or final) fly box against the last set of dividers and install the reel compartment divider against it. Use white glue for this installation, and allow the box to sit overnight while the various glues dry.

Stain the box with a good filler stain, covering all wood with the exception of the inside of the lid. Finish the box with two to three coats of good marine varnish to protect it from the elements, and prop the lid open while it dries (if you do not prop the lid open the two parts of the box will stick together and you will have one of the wife-pleasers again).

Glue the sheet of cork to the inside of the lid, weighting it down with scrap lumber and books so that it adheres evenly, and install the two "fly driers" across the top of the reel compartment with small screws in each end. The hooks of sodden flies can be pressed into the soft balsa while they dry out, before putting them back into their own boxes. The reason for installing these pieces with screws, and for not finishing them, is that after a season the wood will have so many hook holes in it that it will no longer hold the flies. When this happens the screws make the drying strips easy to replace.

That is all there is to it. You now have a custom-built wooden fly-fisherman's tackle box that is the ideal carryall for the boat-based angler. All that remains is for you to fill it and enjoy it. And since you have invested all that time in it, and really should try it out, you have a marvelous excuse for an unscheduled fishing trip.

4

Fly Boxes

Next to the rod and reel, the most important piece of gear in the fly-fisherman's arsenal is the fly box. It is crucial, not only for making the flies readily available to the angler, but also for the protection of the flies themselves. Therefore, quite a bit of care has gone into designing the various standard boxes (I am not talking about cheap copies here, which often have coil springs that do not hold the flies securely, or metal clips that you cannot get the hook under, but rather the standards in the field such as those manufactured by Wheatley, Perrine, and Scientific Anglers).

Let me state at the outset that there is no way in which, with simple tools, you will be able to achieve the same sort of quality present in the aforementioned boxes. A skilled metalworker *could* do it, but the initial outlay for the tools and materials necessary for that sort of fabrication would make the boxes more expensive than the commercial product. However, with a little ingenuity and the effective use of readily obtainable and inexpensive materials, the angler can readily create handy boxes far superior to the inexpensive imitations on the market—and, since a fly-fisherman tends to accumulate flies over the years, extra boxes are always welcome.

The first box we will make involves the greatest amount of construction—which is not much—as well as the greatest expense—about 40¢.

Fly boxes

Bill of Materials	
2 pc. 3/16″ x 4″ x 6″ balsa wood	Top and bottom
2 pc. 3/16″ x 1″ x 6″ balsa wood	Sides
2 pc. 3/16″ x 1″ x 3⅝″ balsa wood	Ends
1 pkg. straight pins	
Ambroid cement	
Cloth tape	
2 pc. art or decorator foam rubber, 3⅝″ x 5⅝″	

Construct the basic box in the same manner that you did the fly-fisherman's tackle box (instructions, p. 39). Glue the pieces of wood together with Ambroid, one of the best glues available for balsa wood work, and pin the pieces in place with the straight pins until the box is thoroughly dry—at least overnight, and preferably thirty-six hours.

Now cut the box precisely in half, creating two ½″ deep trays. Obviously, a standard saw would tear the balsa apart, so the cut will have to be made with an X-acto knife or a single-edged razor blade. I strongly recommend the X-acto knife, not only because of the greater control and safety that it provides, but also because if you want to build the midge vise, you will need the knife handle for the jaws.

Now comes the most time-consuming part. The entire box must be coated with ten coats of a good varnish, or acrylic Zar. This is very tedious to do with a brush, plus the fact that the brush must be

45

cleaned after each coat; so, any of the various urethane finishes that come in spray cans can be used to save time and trouble. Whichever form of coating the box you choose, make the coats thin and smooth so there will not be runs and lumps, and give the box plenty of time to dry between each coat. Do the box both inside and out, and by the time the tenth coat has thoroughly dried the finish should be like plastic. This coating strengthens the wood and makes it waterproof.

Coat the inside of the top and bottom thinly with Ambroid, spreading it thinly for an even layer. Then press the two pieces of decorator or art foam rubber into the cement, and allow them to dry. The foam rubber will hold the flies without dulling their points, and will hold up through years of heavy use.

Finally, glue a strip of cloth tape along one side of the closed box to serve as a hinge. Do not rely on the stickum that is already on the tape; it is not waterproof.

If a latch is desired, small latches that press into the wood can be obtained at many hobby and craft stores. Use glue on the back of the latch, and seat it firmly. The problem with latches is that they tend to work loose after a while, and they do snag the pockets of the fishing vest. The box can be kept shut quite readily by simply putting a rubber band around it. The band is easy to remove when flies are needed, will not snag the clothing, and a few extra kept in a pocket of the vest will mean that, should the band break with age, the "latch" can be immediately "repaired" right in the middle of a stream.

Incidentally, these boxes can be made of any size desired; the size given is the equivalent of the most popular size of the aluminum fly boxes on the market. In addition, it fits the interior size of the fly-fisherman's tackle box in the previous chapter.

The second type of fly box is designed for midges. Midges have always posed a problem for the fly-fisherman in that they do not fit under the clips of most boxes, nor into coil springs, and they are so exceptionally light that, in standard dry fly boxes, whether with a single large lid or even several individually hinged compartments, a mere puff of wind can strew several dollars worth (easily) to the winds and seas. And let's face it, once a midge blows away out of doors, you will never find it again.

A decided advantage to this type of box is that not only are all of the midges attached so that they can be selected individually without groping or fear of loss, but also that the cost of the container is not more than a few cents even if all of the parts have to be purchased, and can, in many instances, be made from scraps from other projects and things to be found around the house.

Close-up of prescription tube midge box

Bill of Materials

1 Plastic pill vial, 2" diameter x 4¼" deep
1 Dowel, ¾" diameter x 4" long
1 #6 Brass wood screw, ¾" long
4 strips art foam, ⅛" x ⅛" x 4" long
Ambroid cement

Find the center of the top to the pill bottle, and thread the screw through it into the center of the wooden dowel, pulling it up tightly, so that it does not make contact with the bottom of the vial. (This assures that the vial will close securely.)

Now attach the strips of art foam to the dowel with the Ambroid as shown. Your "midge box" is finished.

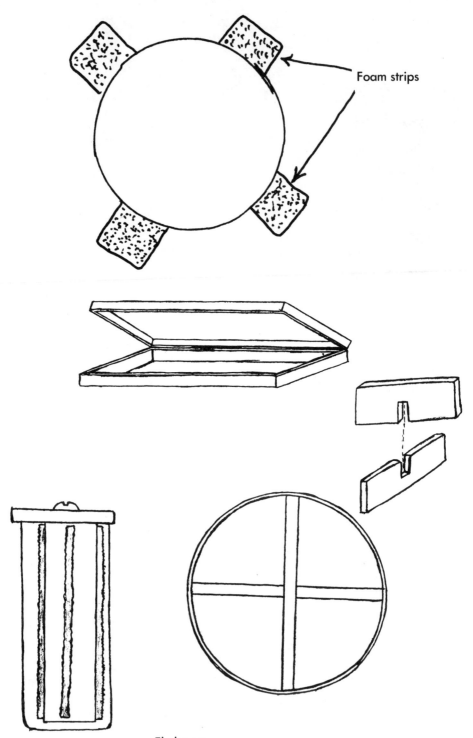

Foam strips

Fly boxes

The size box given in the bill of materials holds four dozen midges, readily accessible, easily visible through the outside, and safe. Of course, any size pill bottle can be used, simply by adapting the diameter and length of the dowel to the appropriate size, but if the dowel becomes too small, the flies will be crowded. Pill bottles, if not available around the home, can be obtained from most pharmacists at a very nominal cost.

The third type of fly box *is* aluminum—and plastic—and balsa wood; but you can "build" it in less than five minutes. It is a takeoff on the rotary-style plastic boxes that some anglers prefer to the standard fly boxes.

There is no need of providing a bill of materials for this box. All you need is a flat, resealable aluminum can of the sort that various "snacking" or sandwich meat spreads come in. After you have finished with the contents, wash the can thoroughly. Now take two pieces of balsa wood, measured to the diameter and depth of the individual can (since different manufacturers vary the sizes of their cans so much, it would be pointless to give measurements for a certain brand, since it might not be available in your area), and slot them as shown in the illustration.

Cut a circle of sheet cork and glue it to the bottom of the can, then, fitting the two pieces of balsa together, glue them into the can, being liberal with the glue so that hooks, wings, or hackles cannot find any cracks to slip into and become damaged. Snap the plastic lid back onto the can, and you have a four-compartmental fly box.

Because the lid to all four compartments must be removed to gain access to any of the flies desired, I prefer to use weighted wet flies or nymphs in this variety of box. It is quite handy, however, since it is very strong, and can be slipped into a trouser pocket for a short trip without fear of it being crushed.

Use your ingenuity. There are many "throwaway" containers around the house that, with a few minor alterations, can be turned into attractive and effective fly boxes, at little or no expense.

5

Fly Storage Boxes

The angler who purchases his flies will be content with the fly boxes in the previous chapters, since he will build them to fit the flies he orders. However, the flytier generally likes to have quite a few extra of his favorite patterns on hand, tied up over the months when he cannot get to the water, and ready at a moment's notice to replace flies either lost to lunker trout or eaten by trees.

Admittedly, flies can be stored in multicompartmented plastic boxes where they are readily visible, and those boxes come in a great enough variety so that any type of fly can be fitted. However, there is a definite advantage in being able to add mothballs or crystals to the storage box to prevent the depredations of the voracious fur and feather eaters, and in most cases the primary ingredients of moth crystals react adversely with the plastic of the storage boxes, either melting it, or turning the once-clear plastic opaque and lumpy.

I personally have never been able to understand, anyway, why any angler would invest in several hundred dollars worth of flies and then store them in a two-dollar plastic box that he could not mothproof. With a very small outlay for materials and a little bit of time, you can create beautiful wooden storage boxes that will not only be an elite addition to your sport, but will also, because they can contain mothproofing chemical reactions, give your valuable flies necessary protection.

This chapter will give the instructions for making two types of

Fly storage boxes

storage boxes. The first is a large box that can store almost a thousand flies, depending upon their size, and has provision for adding mothproofing. The second is a smaller box, which can be used for a couple of dozen deerhair bugs or several hundred regular flies, and which needs no separate mothproofing.

Bill of Materials	
BOX #1	
2 pc. ¼" x 10" x 18" plywood	Top and bottom
2 pc. ¾" x 1¼" x 18" pine	Sides
2 pc. ¾" x 1¼" x 8½" pine	Ends
1¼" Lattice strip (length optional)	Dividers
2 Hinges	
1 Latch	
BOX #2	
2 pc. ⅜" x 5" x 8" aromatic cedar	Top and bottom
2 pc. ⅜" x 1½" x 8" aromatic cedar	Sides
2 pc. ⅜" x 1½" x 4¼" aromatic cedar	Ends
1½" x ⅛" Lattic strip (optional)	Dividers
2 Hinges	

Here again we get back to the basic box construction described in the chapter dealing with the fly-fisherman's tackle box. This will be the last time in these projects that you will be using that technique—after these, you will not be building any more boxes.

Assemble the boxes in the standard manner with one exception: since the boxes are so shallow, in order to avoid running your saw blade into a nail, either simply glue and clamp the top and bottom onto the sides or, if no clamps are available, affix them to the sides and ends with the glue and ½" brads. Since the top and bottom are ¼" thick, the brads will only extend ¼" into the sides and ends. Do not worry about strength, since the glue will hold better than nails will; all you are interested in is holding the top and bottom in full, smooth contact with the glue on the sides and ends.

Hinge the boxes, install the latch on the large one, and stain and finish the outside, giving it plenty of time to dry.

The partitions are made from the lattice strip, put together with glue and brads. As in the case of the sandwich-spread-can fly box, I am not going to give any pattern or dimensions for the dividers, since their positioning will be determined by the type and size flies you want to store, as well as the number of a particular pattern. The box shown in the photograph shows one arrangement that has worked well for me.

You will notice that the partition height is the same as the inside depth of the box. This makes for a tight fit opening and closing the box, and because of the friction the partitions must be glued into the bottom of the storage box. As in the case of the fly box once again, use a liberal amount of glue so that there are no cracks in which small hooks can wedge themselves.

But in spite of the friction tightness, the full height is important. Should the box be accidentally knocked to the floor, the smaller flies will not be able to switch compartments.

Fill one of the compartments full of mothballs, or with a cheesecloth bag full of moth flakes, and the flies will be effectively protected. As the balls or flakes lose their effectiveness (which you can easily tell by the smell), they can be easily replaced—which is a lot easier, and a lot less expensive, than trying to replace several hundred flies after a moth has been working on them.

The second box is made in exactly the same manner. However, because it is made of aromatic cedar, there is no need to add mothballs or flakes, since the cedar itself will repel the moths.

Finish the inside of the large box with stain and varnish, but do *not* varnish the inside of the cedar box, or you will seal in the natural oils and destroy the effectiveness of the wood. The cedar box can have dividers added if you desire, but I prefer having several undivided boxes for larger creations, such as deerhair bugs and saltwater streamers. However you do it, your flies will be amply protected in either of these very attractive and worthwhile additions to your realm of accessories—and think of how much fun you will have filling them up.

6

Fly-fisherman's Vest

The boat-based fly-fisherman now has his tackle box, but a tackle box is a bit heavy to carry over a long distance, and it limits the wading angler's mobility, since he must leave it on shore and then return for it if he wants to move on, or even to change a fly. Fly-fishing vests have long been popular for this reason, holding anywhere from two to eighteen fly boxes, and ranging in cost from seventeen to thirty-two dollars.

Now, all those pockets look good—professional, you know? Actually, they are designed for amateurs, who do not take the trouble to determine where they are going to fish and what sort of insect life frequents those areas; therefore, they feel the need to carry every fly they own. And, with fly boxes holding between sixty and three hundred flies apiece, you can readily see that an eighteen-pocket vest gives you a capacity of up to 5,400 flies. If you purchase your flies, at an average of 80¢ apiece, that makes a value of $4,320.00 in flies alone, not to mention the value of the boxes and other paraphernalia, carried on your person—a value probably exceeding that of the car that carried you to the stream!

Well, it is just ridiculous. Five pockets on a vest will carry an assortment of up to 1,500 flies, and if you cannot match a hatch or catch a lone fish with 1,500 flies, and a purchase value of $1,200.00, you are hopeless anyway, because the other 3,900 flies would not make any difference. The project here is a comfortable, loose-fitting vest with

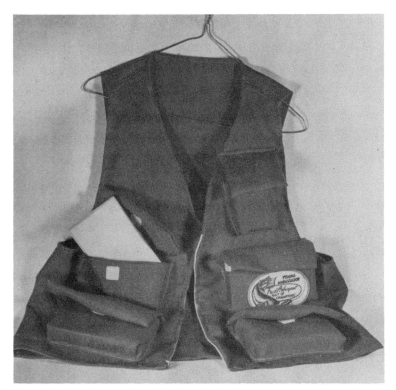

Fly-fisherman's vest

five pockets, and the materials for the vest will cost you less that three dollars. You cannot beat that for economy.

The vest involves sewing, and the best way of accomplishing it is with a sewing machine. With the machine, the vest can be put together in approximately three hours. If you do not have access to a sewing machine, the vest can certainly be sewn by hand, but you might want to check around locally and see how much a seamstress would charge to put the cut-out pattern together for you; hand sewing is a long process, and tedious as well.

For the vest pattern, complete with pockets, you will need one yard of 60"-wide material. I recommend either a light canvas, denim, or medium-weight duck, for ease of working, durability, and lack of raveling. You will also need a 12" separating zipper, a spool of either nylon or polyester thread in the same color as the material you choose, and five ⅞" x ⅞" Velcro closures for the pockets.

Making the pattern is the hardest part, but with care and proper measurements it works out readily. Follow the instructions for making the pattern, in conjunction with the illustration, and make the pattern

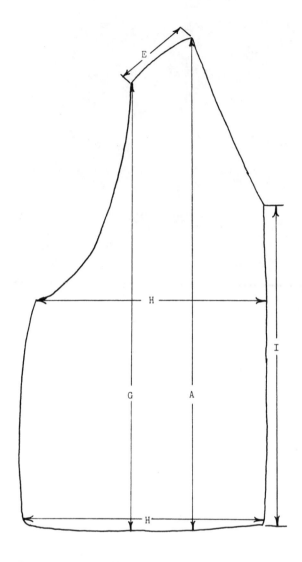

first out of a discarded bed sheet before trying to lay it out on the material. In that manner, if some of your measurements do not work out the first time, you can make a new piece without having damaged your vest material—and you can tape the sheet pattern together at the seams to make certain that your measurements are correct, and that the basic pattern fits. Remember that it will be looser in taped-together form than it will be once the edges have beed doubled for reinforcement and the seams have been sewn together—the important point is that the taped-together pattern not be snug, or the sewing will make the finished vest too tight.

When the pattern is adjusted to the proper size, lay it out on the

56

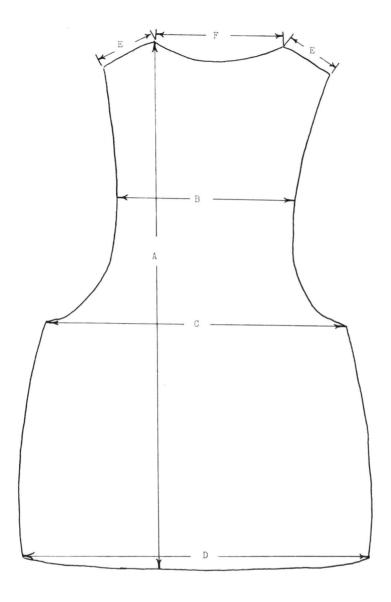

vest material, and trace around it with either tailor's chalk or a Magic Marker. Cut out all parts of the pattern with pinking shears (that will make the doubling and seaming much easier), and on every piece allow an extra ⅝" of material all around for seam allowance.

Because you will be making your own pattern, geared to your own physical measurements, we shall be using a formula to compute each of the measurements shown on the two drawings. The second drawing requires two pieces exactly the same—the second is reversed to form the other half of the front of the vest. The computations for determining the measurements for the pattern are as follows:

Measurement A: The distance from the top of your shoulder to your belt + 6"
Measurement B: ⅓ x your chest measurement
Measurement C: ½ x your chest measurement + 1¼" (for seam allowance)
Measurement D: ½ x your chest measurement + 3¼"
Measurement E: 4"
Measurement F: 7"
Measurement G: Measurement A — 2"
Measurement H: ⅓ chest measurement + 1¼"
Measurement I: 14"

If that sounds complicated to you, do not be put off. Some of your measurements are given in straight inches, and the only two measurements you have to make are your chest size and the distance between the top of your shoulder and your belt.

As an example of how to compute the measurements, suppose your chest size is 40" and the distance between the top of your shoulder and your belt is 24". Applying the formulas, then, the measurements would be as follows:

Measurement A: 30"
Measurement B: 13⅓" (round to 13½")
Measurement C: 21¼"
Measurement D: 23¼"
Measurement E: 4"
Measurement F: 7"
Measurement G: 28"
Measurement H: 14¾"
Measurement I: 14"

Lay out the pattern to your size on scrap material, such as the discarded sheet mentioned above, and cut it out. The scrap material does not have to be cut with pinking shears, since it is simply your pattern. Tape the seams together and slip it over your shoulders. Check to see that the armholes are large enough for freedom of movement, and that the neckline does not rub at the rear. If either of the mentioned curves are not correct, trim the edges until they are, but remember that doubling the material will make them slightly larger, so do not trim away too much.

When the pattern fits properly, remove the tape and lay the pattern on the material as shown in the illustration. Pin the edges of the scrap-cloth pattern to the vest material so that it will not slip while you are cutting it. At the same time, lay out four rectangles measuring 5" x 10".. These will form the four large pockets. Lay out one rectangle 5" x 6"

58

Approximate layout of pattern pieces on vest material (not drawn to scale: see text for sizes)

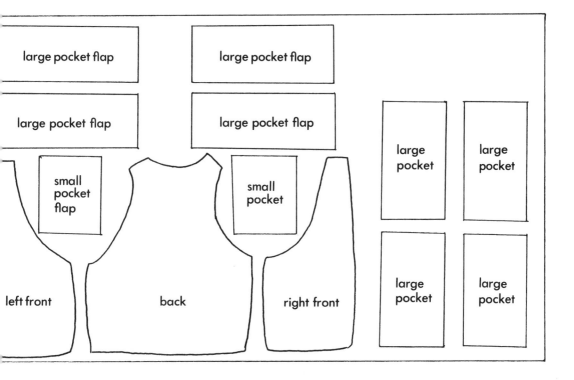

for the small pocket. Lay out one rectangle 8¾ " x 7½ " for the small pocket flap, and four rectangles 7" x 14" for the large pocket flaps. Pin all of these pattern pieces to the material, and then cut out all pieces with pinking shears.

Now fold all edges under (to what will be the inside of the vest, a length of ⅛ ", and stitch the two thicknesses together. This will strengthen the material and prevent it from raveling. Lap the sides of the front vest pieces to the back piece, and stitch with a ½ " seam. Fold the edges out flat, and iron them flat against the material. Check the vest periodically by putting it on, to make certain that the fit is right—not too tight, but not too baggy, either. The seams should be adjusted before sewing. The length can be taken up after the seams have been sewn by doubling it under and double-stitching, and ironing it flat.

Double under the edges of all the pockets and stitch them, making an edge all round of double thickness. Lay the stitched pocket on the table with the stitched and doubled seam facing up. Pinch the corner

Making the bellows pocket

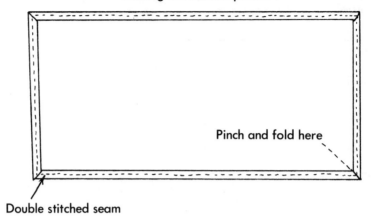

Pinch and fold here

Double stitched seam

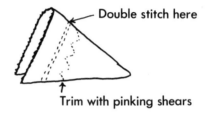

Double stitch here

Trim with pinking shears

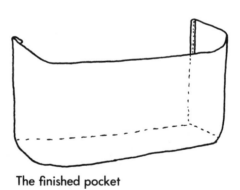

The finished pocket

as shown in the illustration, and fold the pocket. Stitch across the pocket as shown, clip off the end of the triangle formed with pinking shears, and fold backward, making the bellows-type pocket shown in the illustration. Do this to all five pockets, and position them on the vest as shown, pinning them while they are sewed, and double-stitching for extra strength.

60

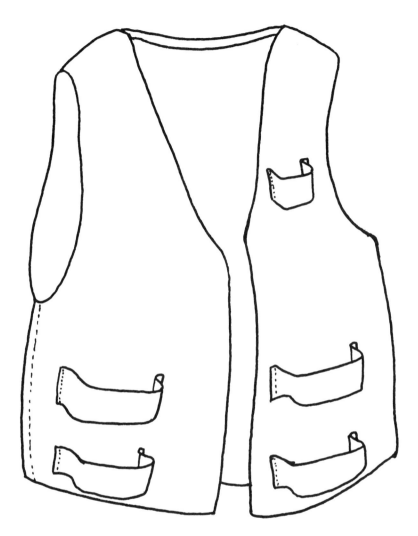

The flaps are made by sewing two edges of the flap as shown in the drawing, after doubling the material lengthwise, and then turning the flap inside out so that the stitches are on the inside. The open end is then sewn shut by hand after the pinked edges are folded inside, and the flap is double-stitched onto the vest above the pockets.

Install the separating zipper (also called a light jacket zipper) in accordance with the directions printed on the zipper package, and stitch the Velcro closures to both flaps and pockets. Your fly-fishing vest is now finished.

The pockets in this vest are designed to take standard-sized Perrine,

Making the pocket flaps

(1) Fold flap material wrong side out

(2) Stitch along dotted line

(3) Reach through open end, grasp stitched end, and turn pocket inside out

(4) Fold raw end inside of flaps, and hand stitch

(5) Iron flat

Wheatley, or Scientific Anglers fly boxes. You can install as many pockets as you like, if you really feel the need to carry more than 1,500 flies at a time; you are limited only by the amount of space on the vest —and not totally by that, since some commercially made vests have pockets on top of pockets. This vest, however, will take care of the fly- and gear-carrying needs of all experienced fishermen. So get it out to the stream and use it.

7

Creel

After sewing the fly-fisherman's vest, the creel will be a snap. This form of creel combines the best features of the flat canvas creels and the boxlike wicker creels. One tool necessary for the construction of the creel that you may not have is a pop-rivet tool. For the creel alone, the expense of purchasing such a tool would not be justified; however, there are many hardware stores and tool rental places across the country and in almost all major towns, which rent these tools for $1.00 for twenty-four hours. If you are on good terms with the manager of the hardware store (one advantage to purchasing all your materials at the same place), he may let you use the tool in the store at no charge. Then, all you will need to purchase will be a package of ten soft aluminum pop rivets, at about 49¢.

The creel involves a little metal work in the shape of forming a light aluminum strap, but all of this can be done with your two hands and a hacksaw. The bill of materials is as follows:

Bill of Materials
2 pc. ⅛" x ½" aluminum strap, 30" long
4 pc. ⅛" x ½" aluminum strap, 6" long
10 pc. ¼" x ½" soft aluminum pop rivets
1 pc. material (see below), 36" wide x 24"
1⅞" x ⅞" Velcro closure

The material for the creel can be the same as used for the fly-fisherman's vest. You do not want waterproof material, since it will not breathe properly to cool the few fish you decide to take home with you —in fact, you get much better cooling by dipping the creel in the water in hot weather and letting evaporation take care of cooling the fish. The only stipulation is that the creel material be strong, and there is a certain feeling of being "properly dressed," as it were, when both your creel and your vest match.

Since the creel bag will be fitted around an aluminum frame, we shall build the frame first. The two 30" pieces of aluminum strapping are bent as shown in the illustration, lapped 3", and riveted. The photo of the creel frame is not done precisely in that manner, simply because the strapping I had at hand was slightly shorter than necessary, so I joined the ends with a plate lapped over both of them, but purchasing the strapping to the proper length will make construction easier.

Following the drawing, drill and rivet the four 6" uprights in place. The pop-rivet tool will leave protrusions that can snag both material and skin, so these protrusions should be hammered flat. A ball peen hammer makes this job easier, since it was designed for riveting and metalwork, but a regular carpenter's claw hammer will work fine. Just make certain that the other end of the rivet is supported on something hard so that you do not deform the frame.

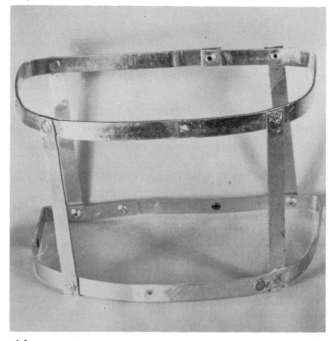

Creel frame

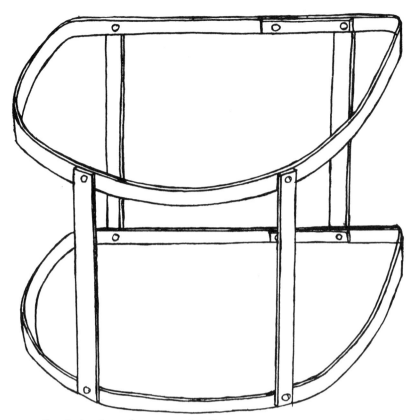

Creel aluminum frame construction

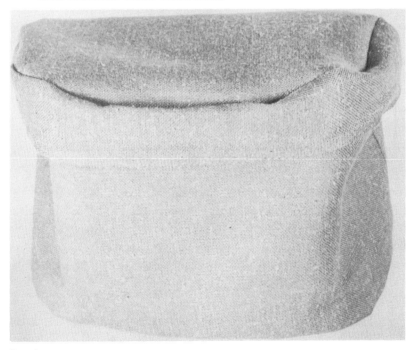

Creel

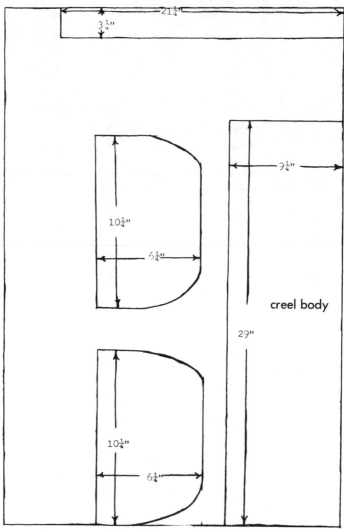

Creel pattern layout

creel body

Now lay the pattern out on the material as shown in the illustration. As in the case of the vest, allow ⅝″ seam allowance on all sides of each piece. The creel body piece allows an extra 2 inches overall height so that it can be lapped over the top of the creel frame.

Wrap the creel body piece around the frame to get the proper over-lap, since individual creels will vary in shape and size. Double the edges, sew them, and then sew the seam. With the flaps of the seam facing the outside of the "tube" thus formed, sew the creel body piece to the bottom piece, with the seam of the body piece at one of the rear corners of the bottom. Now turn the body/bottom assembly inside out, and all of the seams will be on the inside of the creel.

Insert the frame into the cloth body, and mark, on the material, the upper edge of the back of the body piece.

Double the edges of the stitching flap and sew them. Sew the closing flap to the top piece along the curved side of the top, making certain that your seam allowance brings the top to the exact size as the top of the creel body. Now turn the top inside out so that the seam is on the inside, double the rear edge, sew it, and stitch the top to the marked rear of the creel. Fold the extra material down over the frame, and stitch it by hand, thus effectively sealing the frame into the creel.

This creel can be used with a standard creel harness, or a webbed strap can be riveted to the sides, attaching to both the top and bottom frames for strength. Total cost is less than $2.00 (at current prices); total working time—less than an hour.

8

Stream Net

Fly-fishermen should have the best of equipment, not only in function, but in appearance as well. There is a mystique about fly-fishing, perhaps unjustified, since many people think that mastering the long rod is more difficult than it actually is, but nevertheless it is very rewarding to be looked upon as one of the "elite" of the angling art, even if we know deep in our hearts that it is not valid.

So what are you doing with a rubber-handled, aluminum tubing framed landing net? Isn't that sort of like driving a Rolls Royce with a moth-eaten squirrel tail tied to the radio antenna? You should have a wooden-framed stream net, and that is precisely what you are going to make in this chapter.

The wooden framed net has advantages beyond appearance, of course. The grip will not come down with a case of galloping dry rot that will flake it apart in your hand, resulting in the grip giving way in the midst of sliding it under that eighteen-pound brown. The wooden frame is also quite buoyant, so all you have to do is slide it under the fish and let the natural buoyancy take care of raising the net under the fish and trapping it. The net can also be made larger than the standard "trout nets" sold in department stores. And the cost will be less than three dollars, as opposed to twenty-eight dollars for a comparable net through some of the elite catalogs serving fly-fishermen.

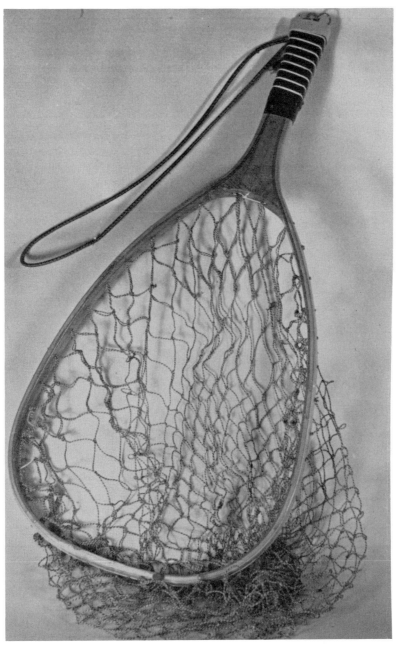

Stream net

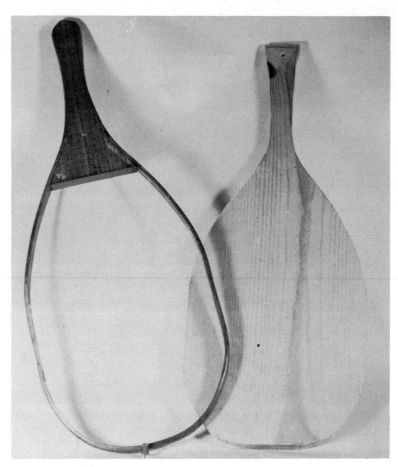

Net frame and form

Bill of Materials	
1 pc. ¾″ x 10″ pine, 24″ long	Form
1 pc. ¾″ x 3″ pine, 8″ long	Handle
2 pc. ¼″ x ¾″ screen molding, 48″ long	Frame
1 Commercially made net bag	
1 pc. heavy bonded nylon seine twine, 4′ long	
Plastic tape	Grip
Plastic lacing	Grip ornament
Screw eye	
Medium snap	
2′ Decorative elastic cord	Lanyard

In spite of the appearance of the bill of materials, the net is actually rather simple to manufacture. Make the pattern for the form on the

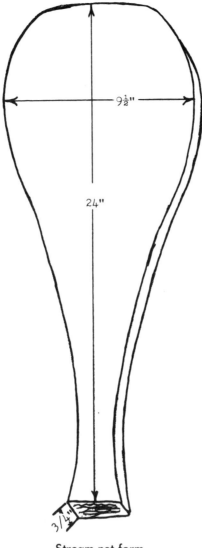

Stream net form

10″ by 14″ pine, using the diagram for the proper shape. It does not have to be exactly the same as the one shown in the illustration—one of the aesthetic advantages to making this sort of net is that the exact shape and size can be an individual thing, so that your net will be distinctly your own. The photographs accompanying this chapter show two slightly different shapes of frame (the darker net is made of mahogany, an excellent wood for nets if you can purchase it thin enough for the frame).

Cut out the form with the coping saw, and sand away any particularly rough places. The sanding does not have to be perfectly smooth —just so that the form makes a smooth taper around its edges.

Now fill your bathtub with the hottest water you can, to a depth of at least 4". Put the two lengths of screen molding into the water, and set something heavy on top of them to hold them beneath the surface. Leave them there until the water has turned cold (obviously the best way to do this is to send the wife and kids to a movie before you start, or children who have not bathed in two weeks will suddenly feel the need for an *immediate* bath). The water will penetrate the fibers of the wood so that you can bend it without cracking or splitting it.

While the wood is still soft, bend it around the form and clamp it in place. If clamps are unavailable, the frame can be tied tightly in place, or tacked to the form with very small brads. Coat the outside of the screen molding with white glue, and form the second strip around the first, clamping, tying, or bradding so that there are no gaps between the two pieces of molding. This perfect contact is crucial, so that the glue will hold and reinforce the frame. When the frame has been formed to your satisfaction, put the whole structure—frame and form—in a closet, or some other place where it will remain warm, dry, and undisturbed, for a full week. (Incidentally, if mahogany, walnut, oak, or some other hardwood is used, only one strip is necessary, and the gluing can be eliminated—it is only necessary in the case of softwoods to prevent damage to the frame in rocky streams.)

At the end of a week, remove the frame from the form. It should now be perfectly dry, and retain the shape of the form. Now cut the handle for your net from the 3" x 8" piece of pine. The upper part of the handle, where the frame will be attached, should conform to the size of the form at that point, and should be notched so that the frame fits into it flush, so that there is a straight line following the edge of the frame to the tip of the handle. Beyond the fitting point, the shape of the handle can be adapted to your own needs and wishes.

Attach the frame to the handle with glue and brads, let it dry for twenty-four hours, and then sand it smooth, blending the frame into the handle. Go over the frame itself with 220-grit sandpaper and steel wool.

Now, using a 3/32" drill bit, start drilling holes through the frame as shown in the illustration. Make two of the holes through the frame and handle, on an angle as shown. Position the other holes in the center of the frame at precisely 1" apart. Apply a thin coat of spar varnish to the entire construction, and allow it to dry. Repeat the

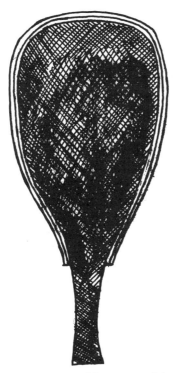

Lamination of two pieces of screen molding around foam. Be careful not to get glue between frame and form.

procedure until the net frame and handle have been covered by three coats of the varnish, to assure protection from the water.

Now take the commercially manufactured net bag (available from the Netcraft Company and several other mail-order suppliers, as well as many well-equipped sporting-goods stores) and lay it in the center of the frame. Start the length of bonded seine twine through one of the angled holes that penetrates the handle. Now take a pin, fly-tying bodkin, or similar stiletto-type tool, and push one of the top meshes of the net bag through the first hole above the one that penetrates the handle. Slip the end of the seine twine through the loop, and tug gently on the net to cinch the twine up against the outside of the frame. Push the next top mesh through the next hole, run the twine through it, and snug it up. Proceed in this manner until a top mesh of the bag has been cinched through each hole. Bring the end of the twine through the other angled hole in the handle. Thread it through any extra meshes in the net bag, and tie it securely to its opposite end, inside the frame. If you have the patience and the proper small gouge, a small

73

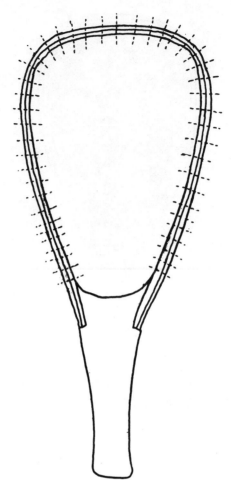

Positioning of holes for attachment of net bag

groove can be cut around the outside of the frame for the twine to lie in when cinched tightly, but it is not necessary for anything but appearance's sake, and runs the risk of weakening the frame if the cut is too deep. The advantage to this type of net attachment is that, should the net eventually tear, rot, or in some other manner wear out, it can be readily replaced in just a few minutes.

The varnished wood of the handle, while attractive, may slip in cold, wet weather, so if you like you can make a grip for it in the following manner. First, wrap the butt 4″ of the handle in a tight spiral with plastic or electrician's tape. It is durable and withstands moisture quite well. Leave a 6″ strip of tape hanging on each end of the wrap.

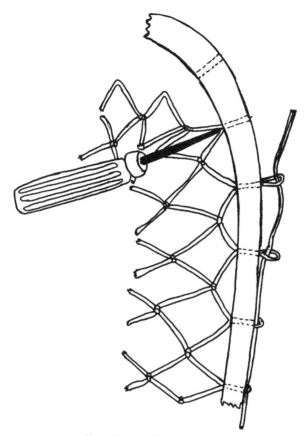

Installing the net bag in the frame

Take a length of plastic lacing, such as is used by boy scouts for various plaiting and lacing projects, in a contrasting color from that of the tape. Tape one end of the lacing in place at the butt of the handle, and begin wrapping up the tape. Coat the lacing with clear plastic Duco cement, and as you proceed with the wrapping follow the edge of the plastic tape, so that the overlap of the tape will be covered. When you reach the end of the tape, wrap the dangling six inches of tape around the handle, holding down the end of the lacing. Trim off the end of the lacing and allow the handle to dry for forty-eight hours.

The butt end of the handle can now be finished off. It can be left open, after being well sealed with varnish, or you can stretch a rubber or vinyl furniture caster over it to give it a neater look. Insert the screw eye, and attach the snap and the lanyard, and the net is ready to take to the stream.

A word of warning, however. As in the case of the wading staff, only to a greater degree, the net on the lanyard, while handy, is a potential danger in thick brush. The mesh can snag on briers, stretch the elastic, and shoot the net back to give you a nasty rabbit punch. When going through thick brush or briers, or while crossing beaver dams or anything else upon which the net might snag, hold on to either the frame or the handle of the net—for your own safety and happiness.

9

Wading Staff

Fly-fishermen are constantly experimenting to discover some sort of shoe or wader sole that will cling to the various types of terrain to be found at the bottoms of streams and ponds. The chief problem, however, is that each of the different types of soles, while effective for the type of bottom for which it was designed, is not effective on other types, and so fly-fishermen still end up doing one-and-a-half gainers into icy water or plunging ignominiously into sink holes that are invariably no less than an inch deeper than the tops of their waders.

A wading staff will not prevent you from ever falling down, but by providing a tripod effect it will at least cut down the number of inadvertent underwater surveys of stream life; in addition, it is very effective in preventing the sink-hole syndrome, since it can be used to probe ahead of you and determine the firmness of the bottom.

This could hardly be called a project, and is included mainly because few fly-fishermen seem to think of making their own staffs, either purchasing a staff at too much money, or relying upon finding a suitable stick along the stream or lake they frequent. The disadvantage to that attitude is that such a stick may just not be available in the proper length or thickness. If you make your own, for less than $2.00, you will always have the proper staff along, and you can make the staff as attractive as you like to be a fitting complement to the rest of your gear.

To make your wading staff (in about fifteen minutes total time), you need:

1 1″ wooden drapery rod
1 1″ I.D. rubber bicycle grip
1 Heavy-duty swivel snap
2′ Decorative elastic cord
1 1″ circle of rubber

The wooden drapery rods are found in all drapery shops and many good hardware stores, and cost a little over $1.00. Basically the rod is simply a wooden dowel, but it comes in lengths greater than the typical 3′ dowel. If you are under four feet tall, a regular 1″ dowel will work fine.

I have given no length for the rod, since that will depend upon the height of the angler. A 4′ dowel is just right for my 5′8″, so you can go on from there.

Coat the rod with two or three coats of good spar varnish so that the rod cannot absorb any water. Glue the circle of rubber (which can be cut from a discarded inner tube) to one end of the rod to prevent slippage on stones. Slip the length of elastic through the swivel of the heavy-duty snap, and knot the ends together. Now drive a brad through the knot into the opposite end of the staff, and force the bicycle handlebar grip down over both elastic and rod.

That is all there is to it. The contoured handlebar grip gives a good hold to the staff, and the elastic can be looped around the wrist to prevent loss if the staff is dropped accidentally. When not in use—as, for example, in very shallow riffles with good bottoms—the snap can be hooked to the wader suspenders and allowed to drag behind in the water. Do not drag it through a forest, however. If it snags, the elastic will stretch, and when it finally lets go it will give you a kidney punch the likes of which you would not believe.

10

Fly-fisherman's Pen

How often have you stood in the gathering dusk during early trout season and fumbled with benumbed fingers trying to hold a #18 fly in one hand while you threaded a tippet through the eye of the hook with the other? How many times, at streamside, have you wished while in the midst of a tremendous hatch that you had a small vise along so that you could whip up a pattern that would match the insects on the water? Too often? How would you like to invest 39¢ or less along with a few minutes work in a tool that will solve all your problems?

The tool is quite simple, and the only components required are a cheap, click-type ballpoint pen and a length of relatively fine copper wire, which can be readily cannibalized from a discarded length of electric cord. The process for making the tool is also quite simple, and proceeds as follows:

First, remove the refill from the ballpoint pen and slide the spring off the end of the refill. Then take a pair of pliers, grasp the point of the pen, and twist it out. Now take a pipe cleaner, and run it through the refill to push out the ink. You may need to use several pipe cleaners in order to remove all traces of the ink from the inside of the plastic tube.

Lay the cleaned refill on a piece of scrap lumber. Most refills are approximately 3⅞″ in length, but you do not have to worry if the refill is a little longer or shorter. Simply measure 2½″ from the point

The finished pen, ready for streamside duty

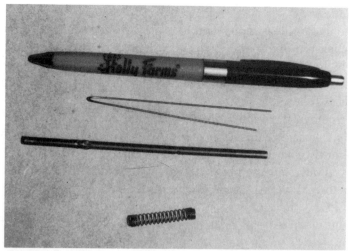

Fly-fisherman's pen component

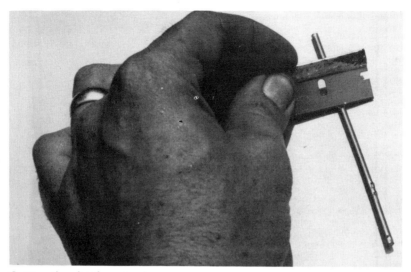

Cutting the slot for wire loop

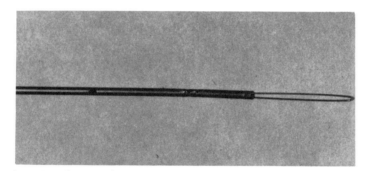

Inserting the wire loop

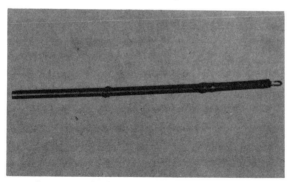

Wire loop installed and wrapped

81

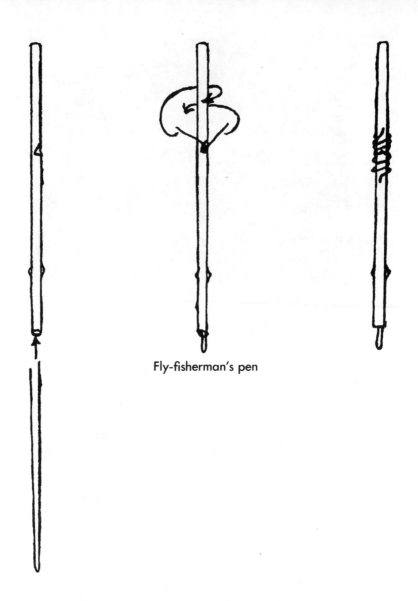

Fly-fisherman's pen

end (there should be a little crimp in the plastic near the point end to keep the spring from sliding up the refill), and at that point, make a small V-cut through the plastic, as shown in the illustration, so that a small piece can be removed from the refill. Be careful that the V only goes halfway through the refill, or the shaft of the refill will be weakened and the pen will not work properly.

Now take a 6″ section of copper wire and bend it in half, but only moderately tightly, so that a narrow loop is formed in the center of the wire. Take the two free ends of the wire loop and insert them in the point or crimped end of the refill, shoving them up through the refill until they reach the V-shaped cut. With a pair of tweezers, grasp both free ends and pull them out through the cut.

Continue to pull them until a loop only 3/16″ in length extends from the point end of the refill. Now take the free ends, spread them, and wrap them in opposite directions through the cut and firmly around the body of the refill, so that the wire is firmly affixed and can slide neither up nor down. Replace the spring, and reinstall the refill in the body of the pen.

When you click the pen, the copper wire loop will protrude through the hole in the end of the pen, and the point of the hook can be inserted through the loop. Click the pen again, and the loop withdraws into the body, holding the fly firmly against the nose cone of the pen, but not so tightly as to damage the extremely fine wire used in most midge dry-fly hooks. Now you can hold onto the pen while you thread the end of the tippet through the eye of the hook instead of grasping the fly between your thumb and forefinger and taking a chance on mashing its wings and hackles. This is especially important in handling the smaller flies, and the fly-fisherman's pen enables you to affix #28 and #26 hooks with the same relative ease as a #8 or #10.

To turn the pen into a miniature vise, make the addition of a very small slot cut into the nose cone of the pen, and, with the hook trapped in the loop, work the bend of the hook into the slot. The slot will keep the hook from turning while you perform the various tying operations.

For greater ease in using the pen as a streamside vise, a dowel can be drilled as in the case of the midge vise described later in the book. Make the hole in the dowel slightly smaller than the largest diameter of the pen barrel. The dowel does not have to be shaped. Simply push the pen through the hole, friction tight. The dowel may then be pushed into the ground or clamped between the knees, thus freeing both hands for tying.

Incidentally, if you keep a streamside diary, as all dedicated fly-fishermen should, carry along a regular ball point refill. With a few minor modifications, this little tool for the fly-fisherman can be turned into a quite passable writing tool.

11

Fly-tying Vise

It would be nice if the flytier could make a general-purpose vise comparable to the commercially manufactured ones. Of course, he can with the proper tools and materials, but such sophisticated metalwork is beyond the realm of most fly-fishermen.

However, there is a major problem with most of the commercial vises—they simply will not handle midge-sized hooks. #18's are dreadful to work on in a standard vise; #16's are difficult; and #20's through #28's are virtually impossible. The jaws are simply too large, and on the smaller hooks, when enough of the bend is in the jaws so that it is held firmly, the hook disappears!

Flytiers have realized this failing for years, and until recently there was simply no way out. Then Veniard of London started exporting their excellent midge vise, along with their Croydon hand vise (which has the same sized collet and jaws). These are beautifully finished tools, and certainly a worthwhile addition to the flytier's tool collection; but there are a few basic problems.

In the first place, there are occasionally problems in getting the midge vise, even with the few importers that do carry it. The Croydon vise, although more easily obtained, requires some time getting used to. And both vises are relatively expensive—too much so for anyone except a midge specialist. The Croydon vise, at the time of this writing, retails for $7.00; the Midge Vise for $13.00.

However, for an outlay of less than two dollars, and about twenty

Fly-tying vise

minutes work, anyone—and I do mean *anyone*—can create a midge vise—a real midge vise—that is just as effective as the Veniard models, and much easier to use than the Croydon.

Bill of Materials	
1 pc. hardwood dowel, ¾ " dia. x 5" long	Post
1 pc. 3½" x 3½" x 2½" pine	Base
1 Standard X-acto hobby knife (5/16" dia.)	
2 Faucet washers	

Find the center of the wooden block by drawing two pencil lines that join opposite corners. The intersection will be the precise center of the block. Drill a ¾ " hole straight into the block at this point, halfway through the wood.

At this point, enlarge the holes in the faucet washers with a 9/32"
drill bit.

The most difficult part of the construction is shaping the post so that
it will hold the X-acto knife at a 30° angle. Mark the angle on the side
of the dowel so that the upper edge of the line is 13/32" from the end
of the dowel. When the 5/32" hole is centered on this line, it will
leave ¼" of wood above the upper edge of the hole.

Drill the hole through the dowel, using the line as your guide while
watching it from the side.

Although the X-acto knife handle could be put through at this
point, there would be no way of holding it firmly while tying, and
no way of making the adjustments necessary in order to keep the hook
in the proper position. The only problem with the collet jaws of the
X-acto knife handle is that they do not always return to the same alignment—otherwise the handle could be epoxied in place. However,
with the proper additions, this failing can be easily remedied.

Cut the top of the dowel as shown in the illustration, with the saw
cuts perpendicular to the line of the axis of the hole. Now sand the
dowel very smooth, including the saw cuts, and round the top of the
dowel so that there will not be any sharp corners to poke into your
hand while tying.

Try the drilled faucet washers on the handle of the X-acto knife
for fit. They should be snug enough so that the handle does not turn
freely, yet loose enough so that, when the washers are held firmly,
the handle can be twisted inside them.

Remove the washers and make any necessary adjustments in the fit.
Now install one of the washers on the handle approximately 2½" from
the end of the collet. Slip the end of the handle through the hole in
the dowel, and push the second washer onto the end until both
washers make contact with the shaped part of the dowel. Make certain
that both washers are in full contact with the wood; if they are not,
use sandpaper to adjust the contour of the dowel so that they are.

With flat washers the direction does not matter, but when using
beveled washers the wide, flat side should be the one in contact with
the dowel. I prefer the beveled washers from a standpoint of appearance, but if you have flat washers around the house, by all means
use them.

Once again remove the washers from the X-acto knife handle, and
attach them to the dowel, carefully aligning the holes in the washers
with the hole through the dowel, using either Krazy Glue or epoxy
cement. Do not—and this is crucial—do *not* try to cement them on
while the X-acto handle is in position, or the extremely powerful glues

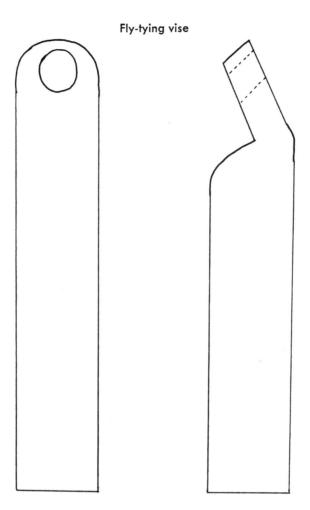

will bond the handle to the vise post and washers, and it will not permit adjustment of either the jaws or the height of the vise.

After the glue has cured (refer to the directions on the individual packages for the proper time, since they vary tremendously) force the X-acto handle through the washers, adjust the length of the vise extension to suit your preference, epoxy the dowel post into the base, and your midge vise is complete. So get out those #28's you bought last year, and gave up on, and get to work. If the hook does not line up exactly perpendicular to the table when tightened into the jaws, simply twist the end of the handle until it does. For an outlay of less than $2.00, you have just made tying those tiny hooks almost fun.

12

Parachute Fly-tying Tool

One of the most important techniques for the flytier to learn is the art of tying parachute hackles, in which the hackle is wound horizontally instead of vertically as in conventional ties. The parachute effect of the horizontal hackle causes the fly to float down to the water surface in a perfectly natural manner, and the splayed effect of the hackle not only gives greater contact with the surface tension, thus making the lure virtually unsinkable, but also looks more natural from the fish's point of view, since insects on the water splay their legs in that manner.

Parachute hackles have, in the past, been difficult to tie. One of the standard methods has been to wrap the hackle around the base of the upright wings, but this method has a tendency to draw the wings together and destroy the cocked angle that is desirable in a well-turned-out fly. Recently, a small tool has been marketed in which the hackles are tied separately around the tool and cemented in place, then removed from the tool and cemented to the bottom of the fly body. This method avoids the problems with the wings, but creates problems of its own. In the first place, with repeated wettings the glue can come loose, and the hackle unwind or fall off; in the second place, the best glues for immediate setting and holding capabilities have a tendency to make the fibers of the hackle extremely brittle, so that a few strikes—or sloppy backcasts, of which we are all guilty at some time or another—will snap the fibers off.

The tool we will build here eliminates all of those problems. The

Parachute tying tool

hackle is tied directly to the fly, and it is·tied *beneath* the body. The tool is simple to build.

Bill of Materials	
1 pc. 2″ x 4″ pine, 7″ long	Base
1 pc. 1¼″ x ¾″ pine, 15″ long	Riser
1 pc. ¾″ dowel, 3″ long	Arm support
1 pc. 1/16″ diameter brass wire, 12″ long	Arm
1 pc. .010 piano wire, 6″ long	Spring
1 16d nail	

Round one end of the riser, and bore a ¾″ hole all the way through, ¼″ from the top of the curve. Now cut a 1¼″ wide slot ¾″ deep in one side of the base, and assemble the base and riser as shown.

Find the center of the dowel, and drill a 1/16″ hole through the length of the dowel, centered in the ends. With your pocketknife, taper one end of the dowel from its full diameter down to the hole, making the taper as round as possible, and finishing it smoothly with sandpaper. Glue the full-sized end of the dowel into the ¾ ″ hole in the top of the riser.

Now bend the brass wire into the shape shown in the illustration, following the lengths carefully. Very slight differences—from⅛ ″ to ¼ ″ —will not affect the effectiveness of the tool, but the measurements should be as accurate as possible. Use a pair of long-nosed pliers to

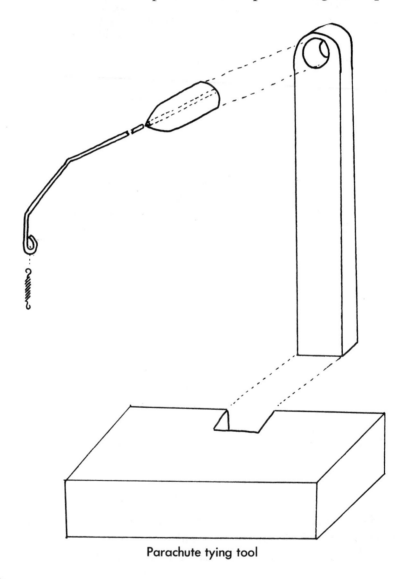

Parachute tying tool

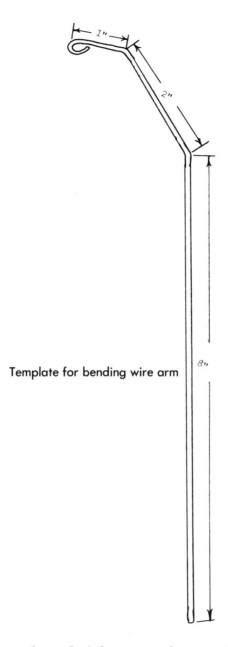

1"

2"

8"

Template for bending wire arm

bend the loop in the end of the arm, or hammer it around a nail. The plier method is much simpler, and creates a smoother job.

O.K., it is time to make a spring. Take the piano wire, and lay it over the shank of the 16d nail, with ½" of the wire extending toward you. If you have access to a vise, clamp the nail and wire together. If not, use pliers to hold them together while you start making tight wraps with the wire around the nail. The wraps must butt against each other, and be pulled as tightly as possible. Wrap until ½″ of the wire is left, extending away from you. Now release the wire *very slowly*—do not just let go, or it can snap back and cut your fingers. When the spring tension has been released, slide the formed spring off the nail and bend a smooth hook into each ½″ extension. Hook one end to the bend in the brass wire, slide the straight end of the brass wire into the drilled dowel arm support, and the parachute fly-tying tool is ready to put into operation.

Because the use of this tool will be unfamiliar to flytiers, its operation is as follows:

Set the tool behind the fly-tying vise, so that the coil spring hangs directly above the hook, approximately a third of the shank length from the eye. Adjust the height of the vise so that there will be a ⅜″ to ½″ gap between the hook and the bottom of the coil spring.

Now tie the fly in the conventional manner: tail wisps, body, wings —but eliminate the hackle, and do not whip-finish the head. Instead, throw a double half-hitch around the shank behind the eye, and bring the thread back to a point directly behind the base of the wings, and half-hitch once.

Remove the fly from the vise, and turn it over, so that the *top* of the shank is parallel to the tying bench. Strip the fibers from the butt of a hackle feather of the proper color for the fly in question, so that enough fibers are left for three conventional turns and ½″ extra. After a bit of practice, you will be able to estimate the amount perfectly, but it may take a few tries before you get it right.

Lay the hackle along the body of the fly with the base of the fibers directly atop the thread half-hitch, and the tip of the hackle extending past the bend of the hook (see the illustration). Make certain that the shaft of the hackle does not slip to the side of the body, and tie it in.

Now make a loop with the hackle stem, about ¼″ in diameter, as shown in the illustration, and retie the stem, keeping the loop intact, directly in front of the wings (which are currently extending downward). Make the wrap secure, but not as tight as you normally would. Now hook one end of the coil spring from the parachute tying tool into the loop so that the tension of the spring holds the loop steady. Wind the hackle tip around the base of the loop, right against the body, for two or three turns, depending upon the size and type of fly you are tying.

Holding the tip of the hackle in place with your hackle pliers, take a pair of tweezers or forceps and poke them through the loop, and grasp the tip of the hackle feather. Release the grip of the pliers, and draw

Tying the parachute fly

(1) The basic fly after reversing in the vise

(2) Hackle stripped and tied in directly opposite wings on bottom of fly

(3) Hackle stem looped and tied in front of wings

the tip of the feather through the loop.

Holding the tip of the feather with one hand, release the coil spring from the loop with the other, and grasp the butt of the hackle stem between your thumb and forefinger. Pulling steadily and smoothly, draw the loop tight. In effect, you have tied a knot in the feather. Place a tiny drop of head cement on the knot, and trim away the butt and excess tip of the hackle.

Turn the fly back to its original position in the vise, wrap a smooth, small head, whip finish and varnish, and the fly is complete.

In addition to the action of the fly on the cast and on the water, there is a further advantage to tying parachute hackles (which may, incidentally, be tied with any sort of wing form—slips from duck or goose quills, cut-wings, hair wings, or hackle points; and with any of the traditional patterns, for better presentation, as well as the newer more realistic forms).

You will notice the small amount of hackle that was used—actually, just a very short area near the tip. Now, look around your fly-tying bench, and estimate the number of hackles lying there that heretofore

(4) Spring of tying tool attached to loop, and hackle wound around base of loop

(5) Tip of hackle grasped with tweezers and pulled through loop; spring released; loop drawn snug by pulling on the butt of the hackle

(6) Apply a drop of cement to finished hackle center with a bodkin

(7) The finished parachute hackle fly

(A) Side view   (B) Top view

have not been of "dry fly quality," because of too much web down near the butt—and sometimes not so near. Strip off that webby part, and look at what is left, in the fine, clean, stiff fibers found near the tips of hackles in *every* graded dry-fly neck. Not enough for a conventional tie, but plenty for the parachute hackle. So, by using the parachute tying tool, you have drastically *increased* your supply of good, even excellent, dry-fly hackles. And that, my friends, is really a bonus savings.

13

Fly-drying Rack

Picture the beautiful scene: dusk is slowly falling over a broad trout stream, with shallow, pebbly riffles that make for easy wading right to the edges of several deep holes that extend under low-hanging trees. All over the water, mayflies are rising, and trout are following them greedily. Your flies have not been producing, but you manage to trap one of the emergent insects, and find that you can match it precisely with a #16 *Iron fraudator* imitation. You scan your boxes in vain, and then, miracle of miracles, you find a single fly that will do the trick. Tenderly you take it out of the box, lift the end of your tippet—and discover that the eye of the hook is solidly filled with head cement!

The "solid eye syndrome" is a common failing of beginning tiers, and even a few advanced tiers when dealing with small flies, especially when they are in a hurry to get those flies into their boxes and get onto the stream. However, with one readily made tool for the bench, this problem can be completely avoided, thus eliminating the frustration of such a scene as described above.

The fly-drying rack assures that no cement will be in the hook eye when the fly is put in the box. While the work involved is of a precision nature, it can be done by anyone willing to take the time to do it correctly, and, in addition to being quite inexpensive, the finished rack is an attractive addition to your fly-tying furnishings.

You will notice that there are two racks shown in the photograph— one plain, one quite ornate. The ornate model was turned on a lathe,

Lathe-turned fly-drying rack

just to show what could be done in elevating the flytier's tools from the ranks of the functional to the ranks of the beautiful. You will see from the illustration that the practical parts of the tool are precisely the same on both models, so there is no inherent advantage of one over the other. It is simply a matter of the type of tools you have available, and what you want to do. Anyone with access to a lathe can make the carved column and faceplate lacquer rack that serves as the base, so for the purposes of this article we will discuss only the simpler model, which can be made with the drill and coping saw.

Bill of Materials	
1 pc. ¾" pine, 4" diameter	Top rack
1 pc. ¾" pine, 5½" diameter	Lower rack
1 pc. ¾" dowel, 1" long	Lower tongue
1 pc. 1¼" dowel, 5" long	Main column
1 pc. ¾" dowel, 3" long	Upper column
1 pc. ⅜" dowel, 1" long	Upper tongue
1 pc. 1½" x 5" x 5" pine	Base
36 Dressmaker pins	Fly holders

Cut the top and lower racks from standard pine with a coping saw after laying them out with a compass, and sand them as smooth as possible, going through the various grits of sandpaper and steel wool as explained in previous chapters. Sand the edges especially carefully.

The hardest and most time-consuming part of building the rack is building the column from the various pieces of dowel. The point to bear in mind is that you should proceed slowly and carefully; otherwise the drill bit can splinter the wood, and if the holes are not centered the rack will be off balance.

Strike the center of the 1¼" main column on both ends, by drawing a series of intersecting lines across the full diameter. Their point of intersection will be the precise center of the dowel. Now, using a ¾" drill bit, drill a hole in each end of the main column, ½" in depth. If you do not have a drill stop for the large bit, measure ½" from the end of the drill and wrap several turns of electrical or masking tape around the drill above that point. Then drill slowly, and when the tape "bandage" brushes the wood you will have a ½"-deep hole.

Strike the center of the 3"-long upper column in the same manner, only this time, just on one end. Again, make a ½"-deep hole in the center, this time with a ⅜" drill bit.

The hardest part is over. Coat the upper half inch of the lower tongue with white glue, and insert it into one of the ¾" holes in the main column. Coat ½" of one end of the upper column, and insert it in the other ¾" hole. Coat half of the upper tongue with glue, and insert it in the ⅜" hole at the top of the upper column, and let the whole structure dry overnight.

Now find the centers of the base, the lower, and the upper racks. In the base, drill a ¾" hole, ½" deep, at the center mark. In the lower

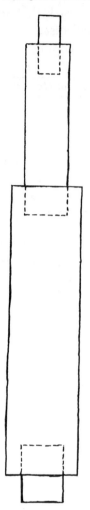

rack, drill a ¾ " hole at the center point, *completely through* the rack. In the upper rack, drill a ⅜ " hole, ½ " deep, so that it does not go all the way through the wood.

Coat the lower tongue with white glue, and install it in the hole in the base. Make a band of glue, ¾ " in height, around the bottom of the upper column, covering the shoulder formed by the top of the 1¼ " dowel as well, and push the lower rack down over the upper column until it butts against the shoulder of the main column. Coat the upper tongue with glue, and insert it in the hole drilled in the upper rack, and let the structure dry thoroughly. When dry, sand it as smooth as

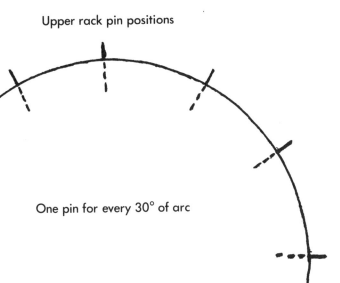

Upper rack pin positions

One pin for every 30° of arc

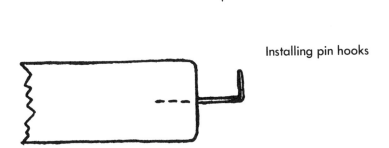

Installing pin hooks

possible, taking care to remove all dried glue that has exuded around the joints. Then stain the rack and give it a good smooth coat of varnish or Zar.

The pins are used to form the fly holders. They are pushed into the wood with a pair of pliers, bent at right angles to the plane of the wood,

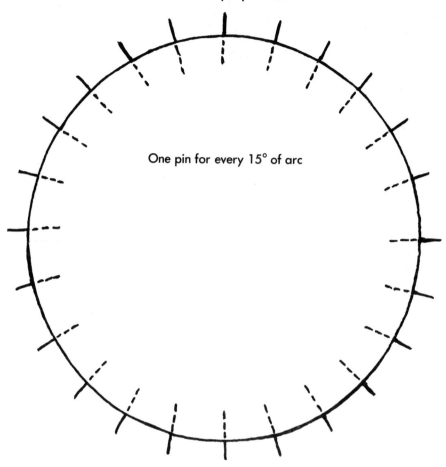

One pin for every 15° of arc

and the heads are cut off, forming strong, L-shaped hooks of fine diameter. (See the illustration for the positioning of the hooks for the upper and lower racks, and for the way in which the pin shafts should be bent.) The rack will hold thirty-six flies at a time, and by the time you get to the thirty-seventh, enough will have dried so that you can remove them and start over again. If you tie faster than that, you are out of my league. Make yourself two racks.

The different heights mean that streamers can be dried on the rack as well as standard flies. To use, simply lacquer the head of the fly, remove it from the vise, and stick the pin through the eye and let it hang. You have a very attractive piece of fly-tying furniture, but what is more important, you will never have another clogged fly eye.

100

14

Line Storage Rack

There can be no question in the minds of any of us who have passed our salad days and entered the main course that modern fly lines are far superior to their earlier greased silk or linen counterparts. They float much more readily, and with much less care (although they certainly have to be cleaned periodically), and the various combinations of floating and sinking characteristics coupled with a wide variety of weights and tapers make the fly-fisherman's previous problems resolve to a simple matter of choice of the proper line for the fish he is going after and the conditions under which it is to be found.

Made of nylon and plastic foam, the new lines are a dream, even insofar as taking out the tight coils that come from storage on the reel. Just strip out fifty or sixty yards of line (or the length of your longest cast plus twenty feet), tie the free end to a tree and pull gently, and the line will stretch out almost perfectly straight.

Nevertheless, stretching the line out is a nuisance. And if you forget to do it at home before your trip, you run the risk of ending up in the middle of a large field, half a mile or more from the nearest tree —or in the middle of trees so thick that you cannot walk ten yards in a straight line. The answer is to store the lines properly at the end of the season, and this project is the answer to the problem of how to store them safely.

The line storage rack is easy to build, quite inexpensive, and a worthwhile investment when you consider the amount of money you have

Line storage rack

tied up in your special tapered lines. The materials needed are as follows:

Bill of Materials	
2 pc. ¾″ pine, 5″ in diameter	Top and bottom
8 pc. ¼″ dowel, 8″ long	Sides
1 Large screw eye	Hanger

Cut the two 5″-diameter circles from a piece of ¾″ pine, as you did in making the fly-drying rack, using a coping saw. Sand them glass smooth, with progressively finer grits of sandpaper, and progressively finer grades of steel wool. Slightly round the edges as you sand. Wipe with warm water, and remove the little whisks of wood that rise with the dampening, with fine steel wool. When you are done, you should be able to rub your hand briskly, and with some force, over the entire structure without feeling any rough spots or picking up a splinter, since any roughness remaining could possibly rub the line and fray the outer coating. Moisten the 8″ lengths of dowel, and go over them with steel wool, for the same reasons.

Now lay out the pattern of holes on the two pine circles as shown in the illustration. The centers of the holes for the dowels should be ⅜″ from the outer rim of the pine circles.

Use a ¼″ drill bit, and set your drill stop on the bit for a depth of

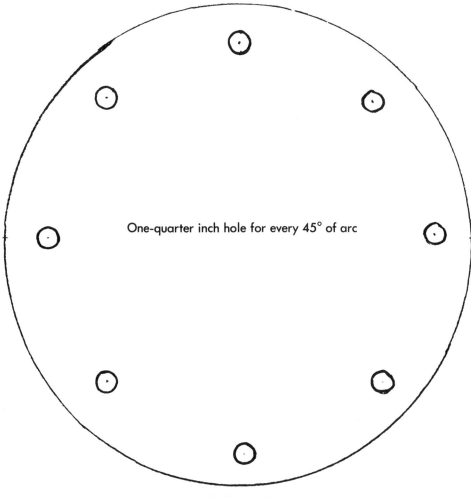

One-quarter inch hole for every 45° of arc

Positioning of holes for line storage rack

¼". Holding the drill perpendicular to the wood, drill the eight holes in each pine circle.

Dip one end of each length of dowel into white glue for a depth of ¼", and install each dowel in a hole in one of the circles, tapping it firmly into place with either a mallet or a piece of scrap lumber, to make certain that it is in as far and as tightly as possible. After all the dowels are installed, coat the top ¼" of their length with glue, and align the other pine circle so that the holes match the dowel ends. Push the circle onto the dowel ends hand tight. Cover the circle with a double thickness of terry-cloth towel or some other thick material, and tap it with the mallet or board to seat it firmly.

Finally, install the screw eye in the center of one of the pine circles, stain, and finish the storage rack.

Lines can now be wrapped loosely around the rack, and air will circulate to keep them dry, while the large diameter of the rack prevents tight coils from forming in the line. The screw eye permits the rack to be hung in a closet out of the way—or the eye can be eliminated and the rack stored in a coffee can or oatmeal box if stored in an area where it is liable to be bumped into and abraded.

Approximately three 35-yard DT lines can be stored on this rack at one time. Unless they are all of the same weight and taper, make a little slip of paper stating the specifications of the line, slip it through one of the coils, bend it together and staple it, so that you know immediately which line to put on your reel when your buddy calls in the spring with the news that a major hatch is just starting on the stream that runs past his back door. In emergencies like that, a body needs to move in a hurry.

15

Salmon Tailer

Landing salmon poses somewhat of a problem for the fly-fisherman.
There are many ways of doing so, certainly, and the salmon fisherman
in a boat does not have too great a problem, since boats permit the
carrying of large nets capable of holding the frequently tremendous
fish. But the foot-based fisherman can seldom manage to carry along
a net of the proper size for salmon—and a net that is too small is
just courting a fish lost at the last moment as it rolls at the angler's
feet.

Of course, beaching the fish is one of the most popular methods,
and is highly effective. But there are times when a gradually sloping
beach is simply not at hand, and there are also times at which, when
the salmon feels the gravel of the shallows on its side, it will put on
a final burst of activity in the shallow water and snap the tippet.

Some anglers land the fish by hand, gripping it around the "wrist" of
the caudal fin and lifting. This method eliminates the need for nets
or beaches, but entails the angler's bending quite low over icy water
in fast-flowing streams and rivers to grasp the fish, thus throwing
himself off balance, losing effective control of tension on the line
and leader, and throwing his shadow directly over the fish, which once
again can cause a final burst of activity and a lost fish.

The salmon tailer project is simple to build, works on the same
principle as tailing the fish by hand, and eliminates bending, thus
keeping the angular in full control.

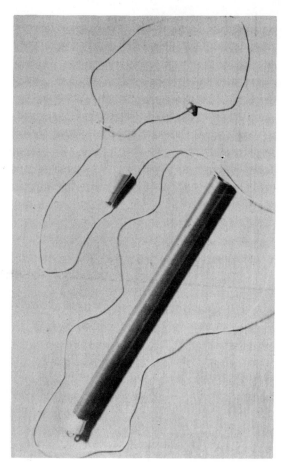

Salmon tailer

Bill of Materials	
1 pc. ⅝" I. D. copper tubing, 9" long	Body
2 Wooden plugs, tapered to fit ends of tubing	
6' Heavy bonded nylon seine twine	Noose
1 Split shot, ⅛ oz.	Noose weight
1 Medium screw eye	
1 Medium snap	

Drill a 1/16″ hole through one of the wooden plugs 3/16″ from the center, and work the bit up and down to clean out the sawdust. Coat the plug with waterproof glue and drive it firmly into one end of the copper tubing. Install the medium screw eye in the center of the plug.

Now thread the length of seine twine through the 1/16″ hole, and pull it through the tube until only 3″ extend on the outside of the plug. Wrap the tag end around the screw eye, and tie it securely.

Now make a sliding noose in the seine twine, and clamp the split shot onto the noose near the knot (see illustration). Make certain that you have *bonded* nylon seine twine, because the treatment it has received makes it stiff so that it will hold its noose form instead of collapsing. Regular twine, even regular nylon twine, is *not* satisfactory.

Stuff the twine up into the tube, with the noose expanded to about 1′ in diameter and the split shot right at the mouth of the tube. Insert

Salmon tailer

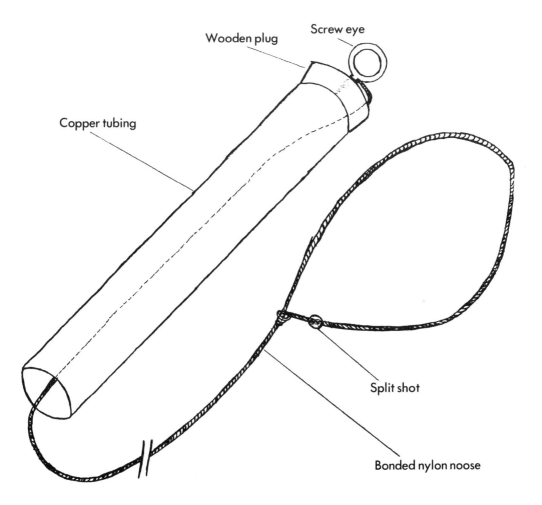

Wooden plug   Screw eye

Copper tubing

Split shot

Bonded nylon noose

the other plug, and press it in firmly, so that it cannot fall out, but not so tightly that it cannot be removed. Put the snap on the screw eye so that the salmon tailer can be hooked to your waders or fishing vest, and the tailer is finished.

To use, clamp the fly line against the rod with the forefinger of your rod hand and unsnap the tailer with the other. Pull the plug out with your teeth and shake the tube. The split shot will carry the noose out of the tube and into the water. It will also assure that the noose will sink below the surface. Guide the loop over the salmon's tail, and lift up on the tube. The noose will tighten on the wrist of the salmon's tail, and it can be lifted or beached, depending upon the conditions.

16

Care and Repair of Equipment

Every fly-fisherman is going to know enough about tackle not to take chances with slamming the rod in the car door or trunk or carelessly banging the reel into rocks, trees, and the like. However, there are many things that can be done to prolong the life of equipment that most anglers overlook. It takes but a few minutes at the end of a day's angling pleasure to assure that the next trip will be trouble free, and I hope, in closing this book, that, one, you will have enjoyed building any or all of the various projects to increase your sport and while away the times when you could not get to your favorite waters, and two, that this final chapter will help you keep your equipment in good repair, so that each day you use it will be as pleasant as the first day you purchased it.

I would like to suggest a small kit for care and repair of fly-fishing tackle. It does not have to be carried to the stream, but it should be readily accessible—and all together—at home, and, as a preventive measure, should be carried in the trunk of your car when fishing some distance from home. I say preventive, because in accordance with Murphy's law and its corollaries, as long as you have along the proper equipment to repair damages, those damages will never occur; but as soon as you leave the kit home because of the miniscule bit of extra trouble it takes to put it in the car, your ferrules will come loose, guides will fly off the rod like steel-colored snow, the grip of your favorite rod will crumble in your hand, the pad will come off your wading staff, and you will do a swan dive into the riffle, snapping your rod in half, at which point the screws will strip out of your reel and the ultralight spool, buoyed by the super-floating line, will go bobbing merrily off downstream.

The kit is a simple matter; it all fits into a .30 caliber ammunition can, and thus is not only compact, but waterproof as well. The components of the kit are as follows:

1 Small can of paste wax
1 Tube of ambroid cement
1 Tube of Krazy Glue
3 4" x 4" squares of sandpaper—coarse, medium, fine
1 Pad of steel wool
1 Tube of reel grease
1 Bottle of reel oil
1 Spool of nylon rod-wrapping thread
5 1¼" Cork rings
1 Stick of ferrule cement
1 Extra tip top
3 Snake guides
1 Stripping guide
Screwdriver to fit reel screws
Extra reel screws
Extra drag plates for reel
Small pliers

If that sounds like a lot, it really is not. For a total outlay of under ten dollars, you will be ready to perform the most common maintenance and repairs on your main tackle—and that can save a costly trip from total disaster.

As for the reel screws and drag plates: When you purchase your reel, it will come with a booklet that tells you how to use it, and how and where to obtain replacement parts. Order the screws and drag plates immediately, even though you believe that, since it is a new reel, you will never need them. Just remember that ten years of hard fishing from now it will not be a new reel any longer, and by that time you will have lost the booklet. Also, once the reel is broken is not the time to be tied up for six to eight weeks ordering repair parts, because reels invariably break at the height of the season.

Care and maintenance of equipment is really quite simple, and should be carried out regularly. At the end of each fishing day, the rod should be wiped down with a damp cloth, and the guides checked carefully for traces of moss or other plant material trapped under the legs. This should be removed, using a soft-bristled toothbrush if necessary. Every second or third day, the rod should get a light coat of paste wax. The wax helps protect the finish from water stains, and also effectively seals any small scratches or nicks coming from contact with trees or brush.

Reels should be oiled in accordance with manufacturer's directions at the end of each fishing day, and the spool should be removed each evening so that water droplets and bits of sand and leaves can be wiped out. Any gritty sound in the reel at streamside should be looked into immediately, since it does not take long for the abrasiveness of sand to totally destroy the bearing surfaces of fine reels. After every two or three weeks of hard fishing, the reel should be completely dismantled and cleaned thoroughly with solvent, then regreased and reassembled. It sounds like a lot of work, but with single-action fly reels there is really very little to do, and a little preventive medicine can save you the expense of a new reel.

Line should be stored in loose coils on the storage rack shown in this book, in between seasons. Admittedly, today's lines are a far cry from the greased lines of yesteryear that would take a set that could not be removed; but even today's modern plastic coated lines *will* take a set that has to be stretched out by tying one end of the line to a tree, walking away, and then pulling gently. Try doing that sometime on the bank of a deep pool while standing in the middle of six acres of greenbrier. It can easily be avoided if the line is simply stored properly to begin with.

Most of today's floating lines float without dressing. However, it is a good idea to carry a small tin of line dressing in your fly vest. When fishing in cress- or moss-choked streams, or in farm ponds and lakes that are full of algae, any line will pick up traces of the vegetation that will adhere to it like glue. This overlay of plant material will eventually make the line sink, and will interfere with casting and line pickup even before the line goes under. In situations like that, a periodic wipe with the line dressing pad will remove the debris and restore the high floating characteristics of the line.

There is not a great deal that you can do in the maintenance of leaders, except checking the knots frequently. Those knots are the weakest link between you and the fish, and they should be made as strong as possible. Also, do not be fooled by the "finest tippet available" school of thought. In some cases, such as the limestone streams of Pennsylvania in late summer, when the water is gin clear and low, then fine tippets and midges are required to lessen the trout's visibility. In other situations, play it by ear—but remember that there are an awful lot of trout caught each year by proponents of the spinning rod, using eight- to twelve-pound test line. Trout, under general conditions, are not as spooky as some of the "greats" of fly-fishing literature would have us believe. And when you are fly-fishing for bass, a leader that tapers from thirty pound to ten pound is sufficient; again, remember that the tournament anglers win a lot of money using line in the seventeen- to twenty-five-pound test category.

The flies themselves should be dried thoroughly after use to keep them looking right and to prolong their lives. A sheepskin pad on the vest, or the rack in the fly-fisherman's tackle box, serves while on the stream, but it can be restored to even better shape when you get home, in the following manner.

Take a coffee can and cut out both ends. Cover one end with aluminum window screen, and make a sleeve for the other end out of a discarded sheet. Tie the sleeve to the can as shown in the illustration.

Now take the used flies, which are probably somewhat matted, and rinse them in warm water. This will get them soaking again, and will help to remove grime and fish slime as well. Put the wet flies into the can, and tie the sleeve around the hose of a vacuum cleaner. Attach the other end of the hose to the blower vent on the vacuum, and turn

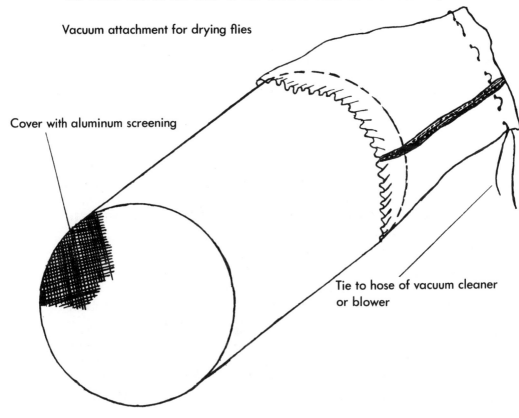

Vacuum attachment for drying flies

Cover with aluminum screening

Tie to hose of vacuum cleaner or blower

it on. The warm air will dry the flies, and keep them dancing around in the can so that, when thoroughly dry, the hackles will be as fluffy as they were when brand new.

A word of warning: Make certain that the hose is connected to the blower rather than to the suction vent. I speak from experience. If you do not like warnings, just try separating three dozen flies, sizes 16 to 24, from half a bag of assorted dust, lint, cobwebs, and dog hair.

That about takes care of the maintenance end of the line. Now, how about repair?

Well, going in reverse order, there is not too much you can do about repairing damaged flies short of removing the materials and tying them over again. If the wings are torn or broken on a standard wet fly, try clipping them off and using the fly as a nymph. Sometimes it is quite effective.

For those of you who remove the materials to salvage the hook, and have been fighting with razor blades and lacerated fingers, here is a much safer and more effective way. You will need two shallow bowls, one filled with Clorox bleach, the other with a solution of baking soda. Drop the unwanted flies into the Clorox. The caustic effect of the bleach will dissolve the materials—and the few materials that it does not affect can easily be stripped off with the fingers. Then drop the hooks into the baking soda solution to neutralize the corrosive effects of the bleach, and leave them there for five minutes. Finally, wash the hooks in hot water and dry them thoroughly. They will be ready for your next session at the tying bench.

Leaders are repaired simply by retying, if enough of the leader still remains usable. Fly lines can be spliced, if cut, but I have never cared for splicing lines. The line never casts or rides the water the same, and I believe that it is false economy to try to repair a line by splicing. Your line is one of the most important parts of your tackle, since it determines both the presentation and the link between you and the fish, and a severely damaged line should simply be replaced.

There are, however, times when a line can be salvaged and used. Those times occur when a branch, thorn, or sharp rock puts a nick in the coating of the line so that it starts to take on water. When this happens, wrap the line with fine nylon thread, just as you would wrap the guide on a rod, starting ½ " on either side of the nick. Coat the wrapping with cement, and let it dry thoroughly.

Incidentally, fly lines that are so abraded that they are not usable in toto can be salvaged. Simply take a ten-yard section of the good part of the line, and make a shooting head. At least, then, some of the line can be recycled.

Luckily, most single-action fly reels (and many of the multiplying reels as well) are easy to disassemble and repair. Do not try it with an automatic reel, however, unless you (1) know exactly what you are doing, or (2) like to live dangerously. Different automatics take apart in different ways, and I am still nursing a scar from an angry spring that decided it did not like my looks. Let the people who made the automatics take care of repairs; they are paid to take chances.

Basically, on a single action (the most widely used action, incidentally) all you need for repairs is a screwdriver, replacement screws, and drag washers or plates. As stated earlier, order these when you first purchase your reel; then if, after several years, the model is discontinued or changed, you will be assured of having the right parts. It is much cheaper in the long run to invest the time and the money now than it is to end up with an obsolete reel that has to be scrapped in favor of a new one.

When you take your reel apart, put the various screws and plates into the numbered compartments of an egg carton. Then, when it comes time to reassemble the reel, simply proceed in reverse order and you will not find yourself holding an odd-shaped piece of metal in your hand, wondering, "Where in the Sam Hill did this come from?"

Rods are the buggers that need the most repairs; there is no getting around it unless you are still using a tempered steel rod.

One of the most commonly needed repairs on a rod is guide replacement. Snake guides, traditional on fly rods and used on most commercial and handmade rods, are relatively thin and malleable, and contact with a tree or a rock will deform them or knock them off. That is why I strongly recommend carrying a few extra in your kit. A guide is replaced in the same manner in which it is originally installed, so see the chapter on building your own rod at the beginning of the book for instructions. At streamside, a drop of Crazy Glue, one of the greatest boons to sportsmen ever invented, will hold the guide on for a few days' fishing, and the guide can be rewrapped at home after the trip is over.

Occasionally the grips on fly rods become dirty, because of the sand, algae, and fish slime that accrue on an angler's hands, and when this occurs the grips become slippery, as well as being unattractive. The appearance and natural texture of the cork can be restored by scrubbing the grips with a Brillo pad (or other pad of soap-impregnated steel wool), and allowing the grip to dry in the sun.

The cork rings used on the grips occasionally crumble, as well. Whether the grip was handmade with cork rings, or purchased ready made, the repair is carried out in the same manner, because the ready-made grips were originally made from cork rings shaped around a mandrel and then removed. If you look closely, you can see the lines where the rings were originally joined.

The crumbled ring should be removed with a rasp, for rapid removal, but when you get close to the rod blank the rasp should be replaced with sandpaper to avoid scoring and weakening the rod itself.

Remove only as many rings as are in poor condition, but make sure that all of those rings are sanded away from the rod butt and from the rings surrounding them. Then take the necessary number of replacement rings, and cut them in half, so that you have two semicircles for each ring.

Coat all of the contact surfaces liberally with glue, and install them around the bared portion of the shaft. Let them dry overnight, then get out your rasp and sandpaper again and reduce them to the size and contours of the original grip. When you are finished, you will not be able to tell that the grip has ever been repaired.

Broken rods are not as easy to mend, but it is possible with patience. Obviously, any bamboo rod deserves repair, and so do all but the cheapest fiberglass rods.

A break in a bamboo rod is almost invariably accompanied by splintering. This works to the advantage of the owner, since it makes a strong repair that much simpler. Mix epoxy cement, and, with a toothpick, work it well into the fibers at each end of the break. Then, using the alignment of the splintering as your guide, work the two pieces of the rod back together, carefully aligning the splinters of one end with the gaps in the other, and forcing the flyaway splinters down into place, holding them there with a piece of Scotch tape if necessary. Allow the cement to dry for no less than forty-eight hours.

When the rod is thoroughly dry, remove the tape. There will un-doubtedly be a slight bulge where the repair was made—this cannot be avoided. If there are any gaps in the joint, fill them with epoxy and let the unit dry again. Then take very fine sandpaper and sand the repair so that there is no lump of swelling in the joint. Proceed very slowly and carefully so as not to weaken the wood on either side of the repair. Wrapping the sandpaper around a small, flat stick will re-create the necessary flats on the hexagonal rod.

After the repair is properly sanded, revarnish the wood, since you are bound to take off some of the old varnish in your sanding, and wrap the repair with rod winding thread extending ¼ " to each side of the repair. The wrapping does not add any strength to the repair; it is just for appearance. The finished repair is now stronger than the original rod was at that point, and the action of the rod as a whole will not be appreciably affected.

The splintered ends of a fiberglass rod, however, should be cut away smoothly and squarely. To repair a fiberglass rod, you need an extra rod blank. Spare tip-section blanks are sold through many supply houses for under five dollars, and since the tip section is the part of the rod that is broken most frequenty, it is a sensible plan to have one of these spares on hand.

After the shattered part is cut away, lay the broken tip section next to the spare blank, and make a pencil mark on the blank at the point of the break. Then cut a 2″ section of the blank with the pencil mark at its center. Coat it with epoxy cement and work it into the open ends of the broken section. Butter the gap between the two pieces with epoxy until it is rounded, carefully align the guides on the two pieces, and allow it to dry for forty-eight hours. Then sand, varnish, and wrap as in the repair of the bamboo rod.

With proper care, good angling equipment should last a lifetime. But things do happen, and if the angler knows how to make simple repairs, and can build for himself some of the accessories needed for his sport, that sport can be much less expensive, and much more enjoyable. I hope that this book has contributed something to that enjoyment.

Index